5.25

NEW KINGDOM ART
in ANCIENT EGYPT

Giving praises to **King Akhenaten** and doing obeisance before him on the part of the **Superintendent** of the Quartzite Quarries in the Red Mountain, the Assistant whom his majesty himself instructed, the Chief Sculptor of the great and mighty monuments of the King in the Temple of the Aten, Bek, the son of the Chief Sculptor, Men.

Stela of Bek and Men at Aswan, c. 1373 B.C.

The truth at which Akhenaten was aiming was, at least, in the sphere of art, truth of a particular and very limited kind, the subjective truth of the senses; it was characteristic of Akhenaten's self-centred nature that he ignored the objective, universal truth which the traditional formal language of earlier Egyptian art had tried to express.

H. Frankfort: in The Mural Painting of El-Amarneh, 1929.

Second Edition Revised & Enlarged 1961

Reprint 1972

PRINTED BY THE DEVONSHIRE PRESS LTD.

BOUND BY C. & H. T. EVANS (BOOKBINDERS) LTD.

© 1972 ALEC TIRANTI LTD.,

72, Charlotte Street,

London W1P 2AJ

Made and printed in The United Kingdom

ISBN 0 85458360 2

(paper)

NEW KINGDOM ART

IN

ANCIENT EGYPT

DURING THE
EIGHTEENTH DYNASTY
1570 to 1320 B.C.

by
CYRIL ALDRED

LONDON / ALEC TIRANTI / 1972

CONTENTS

FOREWORD

Thanks are due to institutions and individuals for furnishing information and suitable photographs and for granting permission to publish such material. A more explicit acknowledgment of this courtesy is made in each case in the *Descriptive Notes,* but the writer and publishers would also like to express their lively appreciation of the special help provided by the following : Dr. Rudolph Anthes, Mr. Bernard V. Bothmer, Mr. John D. Cooney, the Egypt Exploration Society, Dr. William C. Hayes, Mr. T. G. H. James, Professor Ernesto Scamuzzi and the late Mr. George W. Allan and Canon Étienne Drioton.

For this second edition, an extra eight pages of plates have been supplied. Revisions have also been made to the text and choice of illustrations so as to take account of the most recent research.

ANCIENT EGYPT SHOWING MAIN SITES

I

Introduction

NEW Kingdom art during the XVIIIth Dynasty differs from that of preceding ages in showing a wide variety within the conventions of the Egyptian style. Not only did it suffer the normal surface change apparent in the progress of Pharaonic art during a homogeneous cultural period, it also underwent a revolutionary development in its very bases. It would be difficult indeed to define under some broad classification the character of an art which includes such diverse works as the statuette of Teti-sheri at one end of the scale, and that of Nefert-iti at the other (Nos. 3, 124); or the colossi of Tuthmosis III and those of Akhenaten (Nos. 26, 107); or the reliefs of Hatshepsut and those of Horemheb (Nos. 18, 147); or the paintings from the tomb of Amen-em-het and those from the palaces of Amarna (Nos. 29, 115, 133). An art that at once embraces such antipathies as the huge and the minute (Nos. 109, 100), the impassive and the emotional (Nos. 19, 71), the idealistic and the realistic (Nos. 105, 111), the formal and the impressionistic (Nos. 30, 62), the traditional and the revolutionary (Nos. 9, 108), is incapable of simple analysis; and if an understanding is to control any appreciation of its essential qualities, then the complex milieu in which it flourished and had meaning will require to be investigated in some detail. It is, however, outside the scope of this brief survey to present such an analysis, and it must suffice to indicate a fundamental spiritual conflict which underlies the culture of the period and affects very intimately its art.

1

The Hyksos occupation in the seventeenth century B.C. radically changed the trend of Egyptian civilisation. It was not primarily that new techniques and ideas revitalised the tired culture of the Nile Valley, but that the Egyptian now found himself in a more dynamic and uncertain world in which vast ethnic movements threatened his old security. In meeting the challenge of the time, the Egyptian was obliged to change unconsciously the essential character of his culture. The old individualistic feudal society was swept away by the need for organising on a national and communal basis in order to expel the foreigner and expand the frontiers of Egypt so that subsequent invasions could be forestalled. In this process, the amateur who had been such a feature of the old society vanishes, and in his place stands the specialist : for the hereditary district governor exercising a Pooh-Bah plurality of offices, is now substituted the professional soldier, the priest and the bureaucrat. The new organs of centralisation—the civil service, the army and the priesthood—demanded obedience, discipline and a conforming view of life from their members; and it is not surprising that the outlook of the educated Egyptian should now cease to be that of the hedonistic extrovert who had expressed himself so gaily, for instance, in the art of the Old Kingdom. This submission of the individual to a system is illustrated quite clearly in the popular novels of the age. In *The Story of Sinhue* or *The Eloquent Peasant* of the early Middle Kingdom, the hero is still an ordinary man able to determine by his own skill and ingenuity the course of his destiny and to reap material rewards for his efforts. In such New Kingdom narratives, however, as *The Tale of Two Brothers* or *The Foredoomed Prince,* the protagonists are already born to high estate and cannot by their actions escape a pre-arranged fate. They win no tangible success and the interest lies not in how they control fortune, but in how they submit to it.

This change from an individualistic and objective view-point to a communal and subjective outlook, like the transition from a feudal to a corporate state, was unobtrusive largely because the Egyptian with his innate conservatism still kept sacrosanct the forms of his culture. But there were also other forces that opposed this growing desire to submit and conform. An aggressive optimism characterises the earlier part of the Dynasty when under the leadership of a succession of able Pharaohs Egypt expanded her frontiers; and a buoyant belief in imperial destiny created a new dynamic which was a good substitute for the old values of life. This spirit did not begin to regress until later in the Dynasty when a feeling of security and prosperity removed the appetite for foreign wars. In a thriving age of luxury, it would be strange if an egoistic materialism should not be in evidence. The horizons of Egypt had been enlarged for many of her people, and intimate contacts made with the flourishing cultures of the Mediterranean. New religious, political and artistic ideas were free to circulate and sometimes to find a limited expression within the framework of traditional art.

The instinctive clash between these two contradictions did not come into the open until the reign of Akhenaten, when opposition to the political and religious tendencies of the age found violent expression, though in point of fact the revolutionary and the reactionary aspects were in juxtaposition and the revolt has its antiquarian as well as its modernistic aspects.

This then is the main feature of XVIIIth Dynasty culture, that beneath a surface of calm uniformity it presents a number of paradoxes. In an era of expansion, belief

3

in success was tempered with the recollection of the recent Hyksos conquest. The greater consciousness of national unity brought with it the recognition of other great states of the world. The enlarged opportunities given to nearly every section of the populace was offset by an increasing desire to conform to the group-pattern. The enormous growth in the power of state-religion was matched by a more fervent personal piety. Despite the military and aggressive character of the age, the ideal was a feminine one.

In such an environment, it would be strange if Egyptian art, however strong its traditions, however conservative its patronage, did not reflect something of the same ambivalence.

II

The Forms of Art during the XVIIIth Dynasty

Certain trends already incipient in the material culture of the Middle Kingdom appear to have been accelerated by the poverty arising from the Hyksos occupation. Thus the use of the more economical anthropoid coffin decorated with a feather-pattern symbolising the enfolding wings of the sky-mother, becomes general; but though this fashion soon died out for private persons, it persisted among royal burials throughout the Dynasty (Nos. 12, 153). The free-standing tomb statue in the more modest burials was now small enough to be enclosed in the coffin : eventually it merges into the shawabti figure shown in the costume of the living (cp. Nos. 50, 156). With a return to prosperity, how-ever, the tomb statues of the wealthy recover something of a former size and importance, though their old magico-religious significance is now overlaid by the new-found purpose of serving as the official memorial of the deceased. Often hewn from the living rock of the tomb, they are not hidden away in some secret chamber but are placed in the shrine where they may receive the offerings of the pious (Nos. 98, 175). A new type of statue also makes its appearance showing the deceased worshipping the rising and setting sun from his station in the necropolis (Nos. 42, 43, 59). Votive statues, too, become more common as the custom grew whereby the king rewarded a faithful follower with the gift of such a statue, or permission to install one in the now greatly enlarged precincts of the temples (Nos. 31–34, 37, 68, 81). The servant statue was already going out of favour before the end of the Middle Kingdom, but one specialised form, the concubine figure, retains its popularity (Nos. 75, 164–5, 168–169). Figures of servants, holding oil-jars also appear among the toilet vessels of a sophisticated age (Nos. 162–163).

The construction of a costly and futile pyramid to protect the mummy of the Pharaoh is now abandoned, and rock-tombs for both royal and private persons become the rule. In an endeavour to achieve greater security for the royal burials at Thebes, the tomb proper was separated from the mortuary chapel which was erected some miles away in the western plain. Such chapels, which often assumed the dimensions of a huge temple, ceased to be exclusive shrines for the celebration of the cult of dead kings, and became rather memorials to mighty heroes, as is suggested by their joint dedication to Amen. The tomb chapels of the officials of such kings were cut in the nearby limestone hills of Western Thebes, but owing to the generally poor quality of the stone, little relief sculpture was essayed, except in one or

5

two restricted areas of good rock (cp. Nos. 92, 104, 105), and they were decorated instead with gouache paintings on walls coated with mud and plaster (e.g. Nos. 27, 44, 54, 61, 70, 87, 115). Painting of this kind had previously been a second-best substitute for painted relief, but during the XVIIIth Dynasty it develops on rather different lines and earns the right to be considered as an independent art (Nos. 62, 87, 89, 133). It was perhaps because they were untrammelled by exact precedents that the painters tend to be more sensitive to new ideas than their fellows (Nos. 54, 71, 72). Temple reliefs mostly repeat traditional religious scenes showing the king sacrificing or making offerings to the gods, and little that is new is introduced either in the conception or execution of these sculptures. The original compositions of the period, the battle and hunting scenes which decorate the temple walls of the succeeding dynasty, may already have been the subjects of relief in the mortuary temples of the XVIIIth Dynasty, but as these with one exception have been totally destroyed, it is not possible to adduce evidence which is better than circumstantial. Such subjects, however, already appear on a stela, a chariot and a casket (Nos. 94, 74, 149, 150), and the mortuary temple of Hatshepsut is sufficiently complete to show that its decoration illustrates an unusual choice of incidents from the reign of the Queen (Nos. 18–20). Details of the life lived on earth, in fact, whether by king or commoner, now become more usual in funerary reliefs and paintings, and in them must be recognised the emergence of a new desire to leave behind an impressive memorial of a man's life. There may have been more than a hint of the old magic intention behind all this—a desire to re-live perpetually in some other world what had been the finest hour on earth—but as during this period it was customary to make pilgrimages to the tombs of famous people of the past, we may presume that the Egyptian now hoped that in after-years visitors to his own tomb chapel would be able to get an idea of the richness and importance of the times he lived in (Nos. 44–46). While many of the subjects of tomb paintings—the fowling and fishing expeditions among the marshlands, the rich repast and the pleasant entertainment—were included to ensure that sympathetically such joys were experienced in the hereafter also, other scenes—the reception of foreigners, the training of army recruits, the functions at court—seem more particularly to be of a biographical intention, the pictorial equivalents in fact of those personal exploits that two warriors of the age had inscribed in their tombs at El-Kab.

III

The Rise of the Dynastic Style
(FROM AHMOSE TO TUTHMOSIS III)

No revolutionary works such as characterise the sculpture of the XIth Dynasty after the First Intermediate Period usher in the art of the New Kingdom, and there is so little stylistic difference between, for instance, the pottery and stone vessels of the late Middle Kingdom and the early New Kingdom that the intervening period must have been relatively brief. The few works of court art that have survived from the opening years of the XVIIIth Dynasty present a uniform style of purely Southern, or rather Theban, inspiration. Such sculptures as the stela of Ahmose from Abydos

(No. 4), the reliefs of the same king from Karnak, and the alabaster jubilee-shrine of Amen-hetep I, also from Karnak, are so similar to the work of the Menthu-heteps and Senusret I that without the inscriptional evidence it would be pardonable to ascribe them to the early Middle Kingdom (cp. Nos. 7–13), and even as late as the reign of Tuthmosis III, the Karnak reliefs of Senusret I were being copied line for line.

The predominantly Southern bias in the art of this early phase owes much to the circumstance that the creation of the Egyptian state in the XVIIIth Dynasty had been chiefly due to the aggressive temper of the Thebans, particularly to the courageous leadership of their princes. The patriotic fervour which was aroused in the peoples of Upper Egypt generally, found an echo in the local pride of the Theban who now naturally looked to his own past for inspiration. The temples of the Menthu-heteps and Senusret I, who had all built extensively in the neighbourhood, were still standing as the best and almost the only examples of works commissioned by distinguished ancestors of the Theban line. On the other hand, many of the monuments of Lower Egypt which might have provided some antiquarian inspiration had evidently been destroyed or damaged during the war of liberation which drove the Hyksos out of Egypt. These foreign usurpers had ruled the North long enough for its largely cosmopolitan culture, always rather different from that of the South, to become even more distinctive. During the Hyksos domination, contacts with the eastern Mediterranean had become rather more intimate; and it would appear that Aegean goldsmiths, for instance, had already settled in the Delta towns. Certainly the jewellery of this period shows a decided Helladic influence with its use of such motives as the 'flying gallop' and the lion tackling his prey from above (cp. Nos. 5, 6). The character of this weapon-decoration is preserved throughout the Dynasty, the dagger of Ahmose and that of Tut-ankh-amen standing at the beginning and end of a common development. Chariot-building, too, was a craft of Hyksos origin which seems to have been largely carried on in the North; and the decoration of these vehicles with such features as the 'lily,' the palmetto, the marguerite and the scroll-device, suggests an inspiration which is un-Egyptian in its derivation (cp. No. 74). But apart from the minor arts, Lower Egypt did not affect the predominantly Theban character of the work of this first phase. In their mood of patriotic pride the early kings of the Dynasty may, in fact, have deliberately ignored the artistic traditions of the North as being contaminated by their adoption by the hated Hyksos.

Two rather different trends may be traced in this Theban art. The first is the official style, deriving from an anti-quarian study of the royal sculpture of the early Middle Kingdom and already to be seen in the statue of Prince Ahmose—a somewhat formal, classical art based upon an uncompromising draughtsmanship and a prim technique (Nos. 2, 4, 7, 8, 9). The other is a development of the mannerist art of the Second Intermediate Period with its elegant distortions—the wasp waists, heavy hips, elongated limbs and small heads thrust forward on long necks—and is particularly to be seen in the statuettes which are often enclosed in the coffins of the period (Nos. 1, 3). This more organic style develops its own traditions throughout the Dynasty and seems different in its modest aims from the ambitious work of the official schools. We may perhaps see in this *genre* style a vernacular art, uneven in its achieve-ment, yet expressing a developing taste for the graceful and less austere on the part of the rising official classes (cp. Nos. 1, 3, 50, 117, 141, 142, 168).

The early kings of the Dynasty were generally too pre-occupied with consolidating their new territories and administration to have either the time or resources for extensive reconstruction. The first large-scale rebuilding was undertaken by Hatshepsut whose chief monument is the impressive mortuary temple at Deir el-Bahri. This great enterprise absorbed most of the energies of the Theban artists and saw the transition to a characteristic dynastic style. The earliest caryatid figures from the upper colonnade of the temple are in the somewhat archaic, summary style of the Osiride figures of Tuthmosis I; but by the time the free-standing statuary had been installed, the sculptors of the age had liberated themselves largely from Middle Kingdom influences and achieved a distinctive style expressing the new ideas of kingship in their particular age (cp. Nos. 14–17). Hatshepsut speaks of her widespread rebuilding of monuments that had been damaged during the fighting with the Hyksos, and it may be that during such work of restoration her craftsmen absorbed some of the Memphite style of the North with its more elegant proportions and suaver finish.

In designing this terraced temple, it is obvious that Sen-en-mut, who was probably the Queen's chief architect, was at first content to erect a fairly faithful copy of the adjacent temple of Menthu-hetep Neb-hepet-ra, but by the time he had finished the work he had transformed the plan of his unknown predecessor into a much greater undertaking, architecturally more ambitious and unified. It remains to-day in all its ruin one of the most imposing temples erected in Egypt, and almost unique in its picturesque exploitation of a site. The walls of the colonnades were decorated in low relief with scenes showing events from the Queen's reign as well as with the usual religious subjects (Nos. 18–20). Perhaps if the XIth Dynasty temple survived in a more complete state we should be aware of a debt that Hatshepsut's sculptors owed to their earlier work not only for the choice of subjects but also for details of style, though the XVIIIth Dynasty drawing and carving are distinctly less rugged. There was probably more to this than the mere seeking of inspiration from a near-by monument. Hatshepsut was doubtless anxious to clothe her seizure of power with the cloak of respectability, and it was natural therefore that she should emphasise the continuity of her own work with that of the virtual founder of the Theban line. Indeed, this may have determined her choice of Deir el-Bahri as the site for her monument.

Such a traditional influence, however, is no more than a point of departure. The statuary with which the temple was so lavishly equipped, like the architecture, shows the impact of one of the most creative minds of the period (Nos. 15, 21–25). The inspiration clearly owes much to Middle Kingdom archetypes, but the proportions are more elegant and the style less severe, expressing at once the imperious and the womanly nature of the Queen-Pharaoh (No. 22). The powerful musculature and the harsh brooding portraiture of the Middle Kingdom have alike been transformed. The limbs are slighter, the torso more elongated, the forms rounder. The heads with their pointed chins, plump cheeks, and prominent arched noses are obviously idealised, showing Hatshepsut as a gracious young woman with features still fresh and unlined. It may, in fact, have been the powerful tradition created by Hatshepsut's sculptors that was largely responsible for giving the official statuary of the Dynasty an orientation towards the idealistic and the feminine (cp. Nos. 17, 35, 36, 39, 82, 138).

The sculptures of Deir el-Bahri are in various stones and on several scales, and in a broad and a refined style depending on the nature of the material and the function that the statue was to serve. The larger specimens and the Osiride figures are in a conventional official style in keeping with their architectural purpose (Nos. 15, 21, 23, 25); but the smaller sculptures designed for the privacy of the various chapels betray a more careful portraiture and the desire to express the underlying femininity of the god-queen (Nos. 16, 17, 22). It is clear from the mummies of the kings of this Dynasty that the best statues and reliefs reveal the distinctive cast of their features (Nos. 38, 152, 158). As far as private persons are concerned, however, individual portraiture does not exist except in one or two isolated exceptions, and those mostly in the Amarna period (Nos. 111, 112, 142). At best we can distinguish between the portraits of various reigns only, since fashions in portraiture were set by the different Pharaohs in whose idealised lineaments the features of their courtiers were cast (cp. Nos. 36, 37–39, 48; 82, 98; 158, 175). The coffin-mask of Queen Merit-amen bears a closer resemblance to the features of Amen-hetep I than to the slight facial structure of the queen herself (Nos. 12, 13). Similarly, the masks on the coffins of Yuya and Tuyu are more like the portraits of Amen-hetep III than they are of their owners.

This uniformity was doubtless encouraged by the practice of working from casts rather than from life. So far as one can gather from the evidence that has come to light in the sculptors' studios at Amarna, it was customary for the king's chief sculptor to make a master-portrait which served as a model for the greater part of the reign (cp. Nos. 120, 127). In fashioning this model, studies from the life appear to have been made in clay, fixed by casting and thereafter worked upon to produce the desired result. Usually this was an idealised portrait of the royal sitter. Such essays in modelling from the life have been found at Amarna and have generally been regarded as life or death masks rather than students' exercises, since they are so far outside the conventions of Egyptian sculpture. It is doubtful, however, whether more than one or two court artists would have been allowed the privilege of gazing unrestricted on the Pharaoh's features, and it must have been from fairly rapid sketches modelled in clay or wax that the master-portrait was produced. When this had been finally approved by the king, it was probably reproduced by casting so that copies could be made available for other artists working up and down the country on the king's commissions (Nos. 128, 129). In carving statues for lesser folk, it was inevitable that the sculptors would tend to repeat the formula they had learnt in minting statues of the king.

The sculptures which Hatshepsut accorded Sen-en-mut the honour of setting up in the various temples of Thebes, are more massive and stylised than those of the Queen, and the portraiture non-committal and summary. In the pair statues showing Sen-en-mut with his ward the Princess Nefru-ra, however, the artist has shown an unusual creativeness in endeavouring to solve the problem of representing two persons in juxtaposition—but perhaps this originality should be accredited to his patron, for they set no precedents (Nos. 31–34). On Sen-en-mut's downfall they appear to have been cast out of the temples and lost to sight, no attempt being made in subsequent reigns to copy their form or pattern (cp. No. 31). There is one type of statue, however, showing the owner kneeling to present a small shrine, which comes more into favour from this particular reign, the first XVIIIth Dynasty specimen being made for Sen-en-mut (cp. No. 41).

The ambitious and multifarious schemes of Hatshepsut trained a considerable body of architects, masons and sculptors who were well equipped to undertake the even more extensive commissions of her successor (cp. Nos. 25, 26). The statuary of the reign of Tuthmosis III carries on the traditions established by her sculptors but moves ever more in the direction of elegance and conventionalisation, particularly in the private sculpture (Nos. 37, 48). The statues of the King take on something of the idealistic quality of Old Kingdom sculpture, though with a greater delicacy and less vitality (Nos. 36, 38). They are cast in a heroic mould. No longer does the Pharaoh glower grimly upon his truculent lords : instead he gazes benignly down upon an obedient people anxious to pay all homage to their champion (Nos. 26, 39). During this period, in fact, we may fairly claim that the art of the XVIIIth Dynasty achieves a distinctive style reflecting the conforming character of the new forces which were shaping the character of the age. It is a classical art, somewhat reserved and impersonal, based upon that tradition of sure and meticulous draughtsmanship which underlies all Egyptian expressions of form.

IV

The Apogee of the Dynastic Style
(FROM AMEN-HETEP II TO AMEN-HETEP III)

With Tuthmosis III began that expansion of Egypt which was to affect all departments of the national life during this next phase of development. Foreign tribute and resources were not the only imports to turn the taste of the patron towards the elegant and luxurious, there was also an influx of extraneous ideas among a people whose horizons had been widened by military service abroad and who were more receptive to foreign influences. The wealth that poured into Egypt created a new class of patron, often without special traditions to subserve, but with predilections towards the fashionable and novel. The economic activity engendered by long campaigns led to increased efforts especially in the crafts. The furnishing of war-like stores stimulated the bowyers and fletchers, the saddlers and chariot-makers, the armourers and shipwrights; so that when towards the middle of this period a settled era of peace descended, not only was a great body of skilled labour available for the making of articles of luxury, but the wealth was there to pay for them. A bolder use of materials is apparent in this age, and the applied arts made considerable technical advances. The profusion of new materials and processes, in fact, was similar to that which arose as a result of industrial expansion in the mid-nineteenth century and the same rococo exuberance and lack of taste in using them are sometimes evident also.

In such an environment with its cheap captive labour, its wealth and elegance, and its appetite for luxury, it would not be surprising if there emerged that sophisticated ideal—art for art's sake : and indeed there are a number of specimens which have survived from this age for which it is difficult to see any practical use and which can only be explained by assuming that they were made for the sole purpose of gratifying the whim of a patron or appealing to a possible purchaser (Nos. 77, 101, 103).

A taste for such articles must have been fostered by the opulent tribute offered to the Pharaoh at his advent and jubilees by foreign potentates as well as by officials of the

15

Egyptian Court (cp. Nos. 82, 156). Some of the Amarna letters list in impressive, though imperfectly understood, detail the luxurious gifts sent to the Pharaoh by the King of Mitanni on two festal occasions within a few years of each other. Representations in the Theban tombs show several of the coronation or jubilee *durbars,* when the tomb-owner presented the Pharaoh with some rich gift on the occasion of his receiving office, or introduced the legates of other Near Eastern states. For such ceremonies the patrons doubtless demanded gifts that were novel, eye-catching and sumptuous. Sometimes, as in tombs No. 93 and 100, gifts are represented in detail—weapons, clothing, jewellery, gold and silver vessels and the like. Statues of the new king required for service in the cult-chapels of all the principal temples are also shown in these tomb-paintings and provide valuable iconographic information (cp. No. 64). Such functions must not only have stimulated the craftsmen to produce objects of novelty and elegance, they must also have set standards of taste, and encouraged among wealthy courtiers the fashion of commissioning similar luxuries for themselves.

Perhaps the most important feature of this phase, however, is the gradual recovery of influence by the culture of the North; and the interest that such Pharaohs as Amen-hetep II and his son showed in the traditions of Lower Egypt, may not be unconnected with a resurgence in the importance of the sun-cult of Heliopolis. Amen-hetep son of Hapu, the great minister of Amen-hetep III, came from the Delta; and his relative, another Amen-hetep, held the position of the king's deputy in Memphis, while a third relative Ra-mose, was vizier in Thebes. The fine, sensitive modelling of the reliefs in the tomb of this latter functionary suggests, in fact, a Northern influence more subtle and naturalistic in its trends, which begins to influence the art of the period (Nos. 104, 105). Memphis had always been a source of inspiration for relief sculptors, and even as early as the reign of Amen-hetep II details from the mortuary temple of Pepy II at Sakkara were being copied at Karnak. There now develops a distinctive kind of Memphite relief, rather different in its suave carving and flowing lines from the harsher and more precise drawings of the Theban school. That some of this relief antedates the Amarna period appears to be suggested by the stela of Apuya at Sakkara, in which the name of Amen has been erased, and we shall probably not be far wrong in placing its rise to importance in the early years of Amen-hetep III. Indeed, some idea of what early Memphite relief may have been like can perhaps be gleaned from the damaged chariot-body found in the tomb of Tuthmosis IV, whereon the old device of registers is abandoned for a 'cavalier perspective' view of the subject—a space-concept which we may accredit to a northern vision (No. 74).

The most marked changes in the art of this phase, however, are to be seen in the tomb paintings at Thebes. The paintings of the first reigns of the Dynasty carry on without a break the traditions of the Middle Kingdom, the decoration of the tomb of Teti-ky under Ahmose, for instance, differing hardly from the paintings in the tomb-chapel of Antef-oker of the XIIth Dynasty. By the reign of Hat-shepsut, other subjects had been included in the old scenes of funerary ritual; and in the tomb of Sen-en-mut appears the first statement of a theme that was to become very popular in an imperial age—the reception of foreign ambassadors bringing tribute (No. 27). This damaged fragment suggests that the artist was aware of the conventions of Minoan art; and it may well be that foreign influences were already leavening the native traditions. Generally, however, the early work that has survived at Thebes from the reigns of Hatshepsut and Tuthmosis III shows quite clearly that the old convention of keen, unwavering draughtsmanship within rectangular units on independent walls was being followed without any heart-searching. The paintings of this period have a stiff and somewhat brittle charm; the unrelenting outlines are very faithfully drawn and filled in with broad washes of bright colour on a white or blue-grey background with little attempt to render detail (Nos. 28–30). Movement is seldom expressed and grouping is rudimentary, the old device of parallel contours being employed to symbolise a crowd (cp. No. 106). The apogee of this early classical style is to be seen in the fragments that have survived in the tombs of the vizier User, and more particularly in that of his nephew Rekh-mi-ra who seems to have exerted a special effort to make the paintings in his tomb-chapel a memorial, not only of his own personal importance, but also of the magnificence of the age he lived in. The artistic expression of these aims is most successful, the paintings being unrivalled for the beauty of their drawing and the colour and variety of their composition, all within the traditional style of Egyptian painting. In this they stand at the end of a line of development rather than mark a new departure (Nos. 44–46).

A different trend is apparent in the slightly later tomb-chapel of Ken-amen where the paintings are laid upon a rich yellow ground and are noteworthy for the variety and sumptuousness of their colouring and the faithful rendering of detail. They reveal a new-found delight in brush-work which is employed in building up the forms as much as the outlines which define them (No. 54). In the hunting-scenes, the time-honoured subterfuge of the base-line is avoided; and instead the uneven nature of the ground is represented,

18

as in the Middle Kingdom reliefs at Meir, so as to achieve a pattern unconfined by the usual rectangular compartments into which Egyptian composition can so readily be analysed (No. 55). Such scenes of the hunt involved the delineation of a mass of terrified animals against a desert background; and while the various forms, poses and motions taxed the resources of the artist to the utmost, they also gave him a valuable training in expressing movement within mass and depth—a training which he applied to other fields of composition such as the pursuit of a routed enemy (Nos. 149, 150).

This greater freedom is evident in a number of paintings from subsequent reigns, and it is clear that there was working at Thebes along with artists of the traditional school, a group of painters, perhaps not so skilled as their fellows, who were more concerned with constructing form by means of broad areas of colour as much as by bold but often erratic outlines (Nos. 61–63). This represents a distinct departure in the normal space-concept—a moving towards the idea of depth as well as rhythm and pattern, which had hitherto been the æsthetic results of the Egyptian sensibility. With this relaxation, other freedoms were achieved; a certain rudimentary shading appears in some instances, and a more dramatic grouping of figures within a composition (Nos. 87, 88). A desire to achieve a greater unity within a scene may be observed in the freer posing of certain figures which create linkages between one group and the next (Nos. 72, 88). Less often do the various elements appear in individual windows like the frames of a cinematograph film, some are joined to others by unusual poses. Perhaps the most successful of all these attempts to represent a group instead of a string of people, is to be seen in the bands of female mourners that now appear in some of the tomb paintings.

The variety of size, gesture and pose gave an excellent opportunity of introducing movement within a broader mass which is so characteristic of these compositions (No. 106). There is thus a gradual tendency expressed towards a more unified and visual conception of the subject, rather than the intellectual assemblage of parts. This attempt to introduce movement and integration, however, belongs to minor details such as the delineation of plebian characters— labourers, dancing-girls, professional mourners and the like, whose representation had often shown deviations from that of their betters—and we may suppose that the painting of such details was often the work of younger and more in-experienced artists whose hand and eye were not yet fully trained in the Egyptian way of art.

But while the master-painters may have taken their main compositions from pattern-books in general use, there is still sufficient departure from the norm to account for an independence of outlook even in their case. Thus, although nearly twenty scenes of the hunt in the desert, some of them undoubtedly by the same hand, are known from this period, not one of them exactly reproduces the composition of another; and there are sufficient differences in choice of elements and their disposition to show a deliberate avoid-ance of set rules. The artist in the tomb of Sen-nefer has broken the convention of considering the roof and walls of the chamber as the individual planes of a box by covering the ceiling and friezes with a rambling vine. Then, too, in the chapel of Neb-amen and Ipuky, the artist has portrayed the poignancy of bereavement in a most realistic manner by the delineation of a facial expression—a revolutionary visual feature in an art which had sought hitherto to express grief by means of intellectual symbols (No. 71). But on the whole it is true to say that such impulses towards creating

20

the illusion of depth and visual unity are rare, and are only indulged when the main traditional aim has been achieved of presenting a statement, almost an incantation, in decorative terms.

Relief carvings from Theban tomb chapels show many of the qualities of the paintings : similar subjects appear but receive a rather tighter and more disciplined treatment as befits the character of the medium (cp. Nos. 73, 93). The strength of this art lies in the precise statement of its scrupulous drawing, the fluidity of line that distinguishes some of the paintings being necessarily absent (cp. Nos. 105, 106).

The official statuary observes faithfully the conventions worked out by the sculptors of Hatshepsut and her successor. The period provides examples of royal statues otherwise known from archetypes represented in the tomb paintings of the reign of Tuthmosis III (Nos. 52, 64, 69). Heroic sculpture on a really huge scale becomes usual from this same reign and encourages a broad handling of masses rather than a naturalistic treatment (Nos. 26, 78). The bland, smiling portraiture of these colossi, like that of most official sculptures, is highly stylised, expressing the benevolent might of the monarch and his heroic stature above all others.

A more vital art seems to have its roots in the vernacular traditions of the statuette, which served a more intimate and less impressive function (Nos. 50, 80, 82, 162). This is particularly evident in the development of the pair statue showing man and wife in the costume of the living (cp. Nos. 40, 175). The representation of the human form seen beneath regular folds of cloth becomes more skilled as the Dynasty advances (No. 168). Unlike the use of costume in Middle Kingdom sculpture, such drapery ceases to empha-

21

sise the volumetric form of the statue and assumes an independence, though it never attains the æsthetic force that it achieves in Greek or Gothic sculpture (No. 157). But perhaps the most striking innovation is the representation of a mood and an emotion that is now evident in the pose and facial expression of the statuary of private persons. Such a feeling had not been expressed since the late XIIth Dynasty: but instead of a bitterness or weariness in the face of the world, it is an inner spirituality and humility that infuse the work. Statues now appear showing the owner as a scribe seated cross-legged, his papyrus-roll open before him and his head bowed in reverence and contemplation before his god (Nos. 96, 143, 171). The choice of such a subjective form in place of the 'block' statue as an *ex voto* is no mere caprice; nor does it reveal a purely antiquarian desire to revive an Old Kingdom fashion: the faces of the owners lack the urbane smiling expressions of the contemporary official sculptures, and in the grave lined features and down-drawn mouths express the inner spiritual grace which is the desire of the officiant. The art of this phase, in fact, carries an antithetical message—in its official utterances it is grandiose and complacent; in its more intimate moods it is personal and submissive (cp. Nos. 98, 96, 81, 83).

V

The Amarna Interlude—the Revolutionary Phase
(CO-REGENCY OF AMEN-HETEP III AND AKHENATEN)

Despite an influential body of opinion that denies that a co-regency can ever have existed between Amen-hetep III and his son Amen-hetep IV, who later changed his name to Akhenaten, the writer is a firm adherent of the view that all the peculiar features and circumstances of the age that now begins are only explicable if the two kings ruled together for the last ten years or so of the reign of Amen-hetep III. To-day, with the picture only half complete, the changes in art that the new co-regent introduced bear all the marks of a revolution, though it is still possible to see most of their features already implicit in the work of preceding reigns. This is not to deny to Akhenaten the possession of an original outlook. The course of the violent upheaval in Egyptian culture that now occurred, and the characteristic stamp given to it, appear at this distance of time to be the work of one mind, which may perhaps explain its ephemeral nature and ultimate failure.

For a revolution to occur in Egyptian art, two displacements were necessary—a re-orientation in the ideas of the patron, and a change in the training and outlook of the artist. Of these, the change in ideology was the more important. Since the king was the chief patron of art and its original instigator in Egypt, any change of ideas could only come from a shift in the whole concept and traditions of kingship. This is not the place to attempt an assessment of the complicated and imperfectly understood Amarna heresy. Suffice it to say that in essence the new doctrine appears to have had one practical end, and that was the sanctioning of a new way of life for the Pharaoh. The cardinal point of Akhenaten's ' teaching ' was the principle of ' living by truth,' by which he apparently meant, among other things, the breaking with those conventions which had hitherto kept the absolute power of the kingship within proper limits. It was not only that the new king was the traditional living god, there is also some evidence for a return to an archaic concept that he was the greatest god, an incarnation, as his change of name proclaimed, of the supreme and only deity, the heavenly king, Aten. His courtiers bend compliant backs even lower in his presence, and refer to him repeatedly as the god who created them and as a myriad of Niles sustaining all Egypt. This egoism knew no bounds. All the other gods were banished with the exception of the heavenly co-regent the Aten. At the same time as this sun-cult of an earlier age was revived, little respect was paid to precedent. The Pharaoh had broken with the past and created a brave new world that demanded new forms of expression. The conventional and out-moded way of representing the Pharaoh was discarded. He was shown not as a more perfect man, but with all his physical peculiarities exaggerated to distinguish him from the race of ordinary mortals. The costume that he wore was often shown in all its modernity, or as the feminine attire that he sometimes affected (cp. No. 80), though the traditional garb of the Pharaoh which went back to the mists of history was not abandoned (cp. No. 107). Similarly the archaic language of official pronouncements was leavened by the colloquialisms of everyday speech.

Such a change of outlook could not but have its effect upon the iconography of the art of the period and its expression. In the destruction of the old subjects for representation with the suppression of the old gods and their different cults, incidents in the everyday life of the king assumed a special significance especially in the tomb reliefs of the courtiers at El-Amarna or in private stelae (No. 116). In the Royal Tomb at El-Amarna scenes showing the Royal Family mourning over the bier of the Princess Meket-aten, or offering to the Aten (No. 110) replace the conventional representations of the King before the gods of the Underworld which had appeared in earlier royal tombs of the Dynasty. The palace of the King at El-Amarna was also decorated with one scene at least showing the Pharaoh, his Queen and the princesses posed in a family group (No. 115). No temples of the period have been left standing from which we might get any coherent idea of the official iconography of the reign, but the disjointed fragments from Hermopolis and the early Aten temple at Karnak do not suggest that the subjects would have followed the old traditions of royal relief either in matter or style (cp. No. 95).

While there was thus a fundamental change of motivation, the artist, too, was most intimately affected, not only by the novel ideas abroad, but also by the different requirements of his patron. Primarily a craftsman, brought up in a hereditary calling and accepting time-honoured methods and outlook, the artist could consciously adjust his vision only with great difficulty, especially if he were a fully trained man. Here a political circumstance was in favour of revolutionary artistic change. It may be presumed that the vast undertakings of Amen-hetep III absorbed most of the energies of the master-sculptors and architects. The artists available for Akhenaten's ambitious schemes were the younger men, not fully trained perhaps, and not too set in their ways. Thus Akhenaten's chief sculptor Bek, who claims to have been instructed in the new art by the King himself, was the son of Men, a master-sculptor of Amen-hetep III, and both men erected a joint-stela to their respective kings. There is apparent in much of the early work of Akhenaten's reign a certain gaucherie that probably arises from a lack of thorough training on the part of many of the artists as much as from the new and extreme ideas of the king.

The younger artists had often shown an independence of

outlook in their treatment of minor details, and certain trends already evident in the painting and other arts of the Dynasty no longer remain beneath the surface but now have their chance to emerge. The desire for 'truth' or modernity meant that the artist was free to indulge an impulse towards a more visual representation not only in unimportant details and subordinate characters, but also in the main scenes and protagonists of his compositions The imposing of new subjects demanding a treatment not prescribed by tradition was a further stimulus towards a freer and fresher vision. Where scenes of ritual are concerned there is indeed little change from the old iconography; but in the novel compositions there is a complete shift of emphasis (cp. Nos. 110, 116). What we are now faced with, in fact, is a vernacularisation of art. The royal family and the courtiers are grouped in the same attitudes that had hitherto been reserved for dancing-girls and yokels (Nos. 115, 130). They express emotions of joy, pride, desolation, and so forth, not by a symbolising gesture, but by pose and facial expression like the mourners of earlier paintings : and the new unction of the Aten faith is revealed in the spiritualised features of Amarna portraiture (Nos. 109, 112, 124). The human form is no longer considered as an abstraction—a lay-figure with prescribed poses to symbolise a number of activities—it is regarded more as possessing a life of its own, determined by the situation represented. In this transition from an older objective view to a newer subjective outlook, the artist was already reflecting something of the philosophy of his age.

This is the real revolutionary character of Amarna art, that it substitutes a visual representation of things as they appear for the former intellectual symbolising of things as they were known to exist. It is not only in original observation, in psychological differentiation, in naturalistic representation that the Amarna artist makes a departure—the Egyptian had often in details betrayed these as aberrations—it is in a new space-concept that he makes his most important contribution. The philosophy of the Aten cult with its singleness of purpose, its concern with universality and monotheism, finds an echo in the integration of Amarna compositions where the emphasis is now upon a unity of the whole, in place of the former assemblage of parts. The damaged scene in a chamber of the royal tomb at El-Amarna renders in visual terms the substance of the hymns to the rising and setting Aten, and in the process disregards entirely the inviolable nature of the individual wall, spreading its composition over adjacent walls without any hint that they were regarded as separate entities. In the 'Green Room' of the Northern Palace, the decoration is continued without a break on all four walls (Nos. 133, 134). In the tombs of the courtiers at El-Amarna, each wall is occupied by one large scene, in place of the various sections defined by registers, and the composition of these scenes is so managed that a co-ordination results, with the important actors at the point of focus and the secondary figures disposed in a natural spatial relationship. Furthermore, the visual unity of such arrangements is emphasised by a background of architecture or landscape which sets the scene as upon a stage. A dramatic intensity thus informs the Amarna reliefs; the crowds are relegated to the edges of the composition though their members are often individualised, and the protagonists are placed prominently in the foreground (No. 145). That this conscious attempt to render the drama and pageantry of court life is not wholly successful may be due largely to the incompleteness of the artist's vision—the new philosophy still embodied many of the old ideas—but it is also partly

C

due to the Egyptian's methods and habit of expression which were still those of a traditional conceptual view of reality. His changed space-concepts could only be defined by the laws of perspective, and these he never formulated, though he made some shift with 'cavalier' perspective. Similarly, in statuary he never emerged from a frontal aspect of his subject, though a more baroque feeling for space had already been expressed in minor works of the period (cp. Nos. 162, 163). Human beings are still delineated in all the conventions of a primitive style which had been fixed at an early stage of development during the first dynasties, though statues of human beings had been correctly drawn in perspective in the tomb of Rekh-mi-ra a century earlier. The eye is still shown front view in a face drawn in profile. When we speak of 'naturalism' in Amarna art it must be understood as only within the Egyptian conventions.

The revolutionary character of Amarna art appears from the start—the most extreme manifestations of the new style, the caryatid figures from the Aten temple at Karnak belong to the earliest years of the co-regency (Nos. 107–109). The mannerism of this initial phase, unlike that of any other in the history of human culture, can owe its peculiar character only to the ideas of one individual—Akhenaten himself. It is unthinkable that any artist, fully trained or otherwise, would have dared to produce such outrageous departures from the idealistic conception of Pharaonic sculpture without strong prompting from his patron; and, in fact, the earliest reliefs of the reign show the young co-regent in the unexceptional art-style of the reign of Amen-hetep III (cp. Nos. 105, 139). Perhaps, therefore, we should not look further than Akhenaten himself for the chief Court artist of the reign, the instructor of such lesser men as the master-sculptor Bek. The bodily peculiarities of the king have been

28

exaggerated to the extent of becoming a fashionable distortion, a mark of the elect, which is duly assumed by his faithful followers also. Even in earlier times, whenever the sanctions of an idealistic orthodoxy were lifted, the Egyptian artist had often tended to the extreme of caricature in his representations of servants, foreigners, dwarfs, and other menials, for example : and now with the old inhibitions removed or suspended by the new ideology, the attempt to render reality encouraged an excess, especially from hands not fully expert (Nos. 116, 132). The boundary stelæ at El-Amarna, and the tomb reliefs from the same region, with their more plastic modelling in plaster over a friable rock core, express this new-won verve and freedom and dramatic exaggeration to the greatest extent, and are the counterparts of the expressionistic statuary from Karnak (Nos. 110–112).

The artists engaged on the contemporary work of Amen-hetep III betray little of the Amarna influence. The reliefs from the tomb of Kheruef, for instance, though unusual in subject matter, are executed in the same conventional style as those of Kha-em-het and Surer, with perhaps even greater refinement in the carving (cp. Nos. 85, 92). The only traces of the impact of the revolutionary art upon the traditional style are to be seen in small details such as the perforation of the ear-lobe or the indication of creases in the neck (cp. No. 131). There are, however, a small number of examples which reveal more of the direct influence of the unflattering realism of the Amarna style, though these may have been produced by artists working for Akhenaten rather than Amen-hetep III (No. 80). In the reliefs in the tomb of Ra-mose which date from the earliest years of the co-regency, we can see the arrival of the new revolutionary art upon the scene where it stands awkwardly by the side of work in the traditional idiom (Nos. 104–106). The change is more marked in content than in style as the master-draughts-man turns his pen to the delineation of the new subjects in the new manner with rather more skill than conviction.

With the removal of the Court from Thebes to the virgin ground of El-Amarna, where no monuments already existed to hold up the example of the Past, all compromise could be rejected, and the new excess allowed free rein (Nos. 95, 110, 112, 115–116).

VI

The Amarna Interlude—the Later Phase
(REIGN OF AKHENATEN AND CO-REGENCY OF SMENKH-KA-RA)

In the last years of his life, Amen-hetep III, whose health was evidently failing, seems to have played a diminishing part in the affairs of his realm. Coinciding with his third jubilee, his son appears to have announced new changes in the Aten doctrines, emphasising the incorporeal and mono-theistic nature of his deity. With his assumption of supreme power on the death of his father two years later, Akhenaten prescribed rival cults, particularly that of Amen of Thebes. This interdict and the cessation of work on his father's vast undertakings at Thebes and elsewhere must have thrown out of employment a large body of craftsmen, many of whom would drift to the new capital. It may have been such a sudden influx of highly skilled labour that accounts for a more felicitous and traditional touch in later Amarna art, though the master-draughtsmen would hardly have been displaced by the newcomers, and possibly the mannerism of the early style had already achieved a certain sanctity by constant repetition. Nevertheless, the removal of the household of the Queen Mother Tiy, for instance, to El-Amarna, and with it her own craftsmen such as the master-sculptor Yuti, must have introduced more conservative influences.

A less intransigeant feeling is evident in the sculpture of the period which is well represented in the finds from the studios at El-Amarna (Nos. 117–121, 123–124). For the most part these consist of portrait heads of members of the royal family at the end of the reign of Akhenaten. Besides sculpture in stone, a fair number of plaster-casts of art-works have also survived (Nos. 128, 129). Some of the masks appear to have been cast from clay or wax studies modelled rapidly from the life, and are in process of conversion to a more conventionalised representation (No. 123). The elongated heads of the princesses are the only features surviving from the earlier exaggerated style; and on the whole these workshop pieces reveal a somewhat idealised naturalism (Nos. 113, 114, 119, 120, 138). It is these works more than anything else which have given Amarna art the reputation of drawing its inspiration from an original observation of nature, when in point of fact the earlier Amarna style, despite its visual intention, shows an even more extreme mannerism than the conventions it sought to replace. The 'naturalism' of the later years of Akhenaten's reign had already appeared in his father's lifetime, and was only developed after the interruption caused by the early revolutionary style (Nos. 82, 162).

It is primarily in the field of sculpture that we are able to trace the development of this later art. The Amarna tomb reliefs are mostly to be dated to the earlier years: such later tombs as those of Huya, Mery-ra II, and Mahu show somewhat hastily executed work by sculptors still carving in the early manner which may already have been considered the proper fashion for tomb relief by the humbler

31

followers of the king. Even so, each of these tombs, and particularly the last, reveals the essential Amarna traits of a unity of subject-matter and an original and lively presentation. A precious example of later relief, apart from the Brooklyn sculptor's-model (No. 131), is the small coloured slab at Berlin, showing a young king and queen, which displays the same naturalistic treatment in the pose and drawing as characterises the studio sculptures, though the convention is traditionally conceptual (No. 130). The paintings from the Northern Palace similarly betray the same unresolved conflict between tradition and revolution. The choice of subject—pure landscape, observed with love for its own qualities—is as novel as the feeling for space in which it has been conceived, and the treatment of it in visual terms is in the later naturalistic style; but much of the detail, the water, for instance, and the bird-life, is still drawn in the old conventions (Nos. 133, 134).

On the whole, the work of this later phase lacks some of the rapture and vigour of the revolutionary style as well as its excesses. Perhaps in this it reflects that compromise with tradition which is the main political feature of the last years of Akhenaten's reign.

VII

The Amarna Interlude—the Aftermath and the Reaction
(FROM TUT-ANKH-AMEN TO HOREMHEB)

The return to a limited orthodoxy under Tut-ankh-amen wrought no violent change in the artistic climate. The inscription on one of his tomb sealings, describing him as having spent his life in fashioning images of the gods, may well form his epitaph. During his reign there must have been considerable artistic activity, owing to the need for repairing and re-endowing temples all over the country, though most of his work was usurped or completed by his successors.

Tut-ankh-amen appears in every way to have attempted a return to the ideals of his father Amen-hetep III, the worship of the Aten reverting to its old status of a court religion, and Amen recovering his position as supreme state god (cp. No. 151). But while in its restraint, elegance and taste for luxury the art of the period has affinities with that of Amen-hetep III, it is clearly a development of the no less opulent late Amarna style. The cult statues from the King's tomb, for example, show the characterisitc slender limbs and heavy hips of Amarna art (Nos. 157, 159). And while some of these may have been made earlier for Smenkh-ka-ra, the theme and treatment of the decorations on Tut-ankh-amen's personal effects are still in the intimate Amarna mood (Nos. 154, 160).

The statuary of the period is in a refined rather than a vigorous style, expressing a generally naturalistic aim; and concessions to the Amarna ideal of 'truth' are to be seen in the careful delineation of clothing and accoutrements (Nos. 170, 175). Apart from the lion of Soleb (No. 151), the masterpieces are greatly mutilated; but the fragmentary statue of Min-nakht and his wife, and the head of an unknown man, both at Cairo (Cat. Nos. 779, 849), are still impressive even in their ruin. The pair statue in the British Museum is also most probably to be dated to this period (No. 175). Relief sculpture is best represented in the fragments from destroyed Memphite tombs, particularly from that of Horemheb (Nos. 144–148). The scenes of everyday life in these reliefs show all the verve of the earlier Amarna style with the refinement and assurance of the later work. While the old conventional religious subjects showing an after-life in the Field of Reeds are perhaps less felicitously drawn and proportioned, the decoration of this tomb of Horemheb must be regarded as representing the high-water mark of Egyptian relief sculpture in any age. The Boston fragment from a statue of Ay suggests that the same traditions persisted for some time (No. 173).

Painting during this period is uneven in quality; but as the only examples to have survived are at Thebes, it may be that they represent a somewhat provincial and less whole-hearted expression of the Amarna spirit, since it is Memphis that appears to have been the more important capital at this date. The miniatures from the coffer of Tut-ankh-amen, which may not be of Theban manufacture, are technically superb, and show in their design the Amarna taste for a unity of subject matter rather than a juxtaposition of parts (Nos. 149, 150). The wall-paintings in the royal tomb, dating from the first months of Ay's reign, and those in the tomb of Huy, which may be by the same hand, show a certain haste and carelessness, though the design and colouring are often attractive. The later tomb of Nefer-hetep, like the Theban tomb of his patron Ay, shows a pastiche of Amarna and orthodox elements : there is a loss of vigour and some of the Ramesside mannerisms are already anticipated. That the essential spirit of Amarna was still active, however, even late in the reign of Tut-ankh-amen is seen in the design of his quartzite sarcophagus with its novel space-concept expressed in the disposition of the guardian goddesses (No. 157). This, if nothing else, should encourage the view that the court art of this period was not a withering of the Amarna bloom, but its late flowering.

Unorthodox elements in Egyptian art were steadily purged from it during the reigns of the successors of Tut-ankh-amen, and particularly by Horemheb who returned to the well-tried political and religious policies of the past and attempted to restore order and prosperity in a country demoralised by the failure of the Amarna experiment. The art of the remaining years of the XVIIIth Dynasty marks no distinct cleavage with what had preceded it, partly because of the wholesale usurpation of the work of Tut-ankh-amen, and partly because the artists of the period were all thoroughly grounded in the late Amarna style which had come to be accepted as normal, particularly in its proportions and more up-to-date iconography. The pathological representation of the human form was, of course, discarded and with it went much of the fervour of its expression and its sense of movement. The transformation is complete in the mythological scenes in the Theban tomb of Horemheb, which compared with the reliefs on the gilded shrines of Tut-ankh-amen are rigidly formal and already obsessed by the dark that Akhenaten's sun-cult had tried to dispel.

VIII

Postscript

The New Kingdom is usually taken to extend from the end of the XVIIth to the beginning of the XXIst Dynasty. This survey has been limited to the art of the XVIIIth Dynasty not only because the wealth and importance of the material demand a fuller treatment, but also because the period is complete in itself, presenting a beginning, a middle and an end. The Dynasty saw the rise of the Egyptian state to power and magnificence under the leadership of its warlike Theban princes, and with it the great increase in the wealth and influence of the Theban god Amen. The attempt by Akhenaten to dispense the old absolute power of the sun-kings of an earlier age, even when it challenged the new forces within the state, ended in failure and disorder, and his successors were left to struggle back to the main stream of development. The advent of the XIXth Dynasty marks a distinct change in Egyptian culture which no longer found itself in an expansionist phase but was on the verge of a long retraction in the face of new and virile challenges from without. The art of the remaining dynasties of the New Kingdom is therefore better regarded as forming a prelude to Late Period work than as an organic development of the work of the XVIIIth Dynasty.

AN OUTLINE OF THE HISTORICAL BACKGROUND OF THE XVIIITH DYNASTY

About 1680 B.C. the Hyksos, or Shepherd Kings, a largely Semitic people who had infiltrated into the pasture lands of the Delta during the troubled reigns of the later Middle Kingdom, managed to secure the supreme power and ruled as Pharaohs over most of Lower and Middle Egypt, as well as Southern Palestine. Upper Egypt, however, succeeded in preserving some of the old continuity of native government under a family of princes ruling from Thebes. During the later part of the XVIIth Dynasty, a more aggressive Theban family began to challenge the authority of the Hyksos kings and started a long and bitter war of liberation against them and their collaborators. During this period a number of novelties were introduced from Asia including the horse-drawn chariot and other weapons, bronze, different breeds of cattle, the olive and pomegranate, and new kinds of musical instruments.

THE RISE OF IMPERIAL EGYPT, 1570–1436 B.C.

Reigns of Ahmose I 1570–1546; Amen-hetep I, 1546–1526; Tuthmosis I, 1526–1508; Tuthmosis II, 1508–1490; Hatshepsut, 1489–1469; Tuthmosis III, 1490–1436.

The capture of Avaris the Hyksos stronghold near Tanis, the expulsion of the foreigner from Egypt, and the characteristic pattern given to the kingship during the XVIIIth Dynasty were all the work of Ahmose I. His policy of safeguarding the frontiers by large-scale raiding expeditions into Palestine and Syria was followed by his two immediate successors.

Tuthmosis I was not of the pure blood royal and came to the throne only by virtue of his marriage with the royal heiress Queen Ahmose. When she died, he associated the next heiress, their daughter Hatshepsut, in the kingship by marrying her to his co-regent Tuthmosis II who later attained to sole rule for a few years. On his death, Hatshepsut exercised the regency during the minority of her step-son Tuthmosis III, whose claim to the throne had been recognised by the oracle of the god Amen-ra of Thebes, and who was doubtless married to the next heiress. Hatshepsut, however, soon took over the entire government of the realm and thrust Tuthmosis III into the background. She ruled as sole monarch with the help of able officials, such as the Steward of Amen, Sen-en-mut, having herself depicted in the male attire of a Pharaoh. During her reign, a peaceful policy of consolidation was followed : the country was reorganised and temples which had stood in ruins since the fighting with the Hyksos were rebuilt.

After some twenty years of retirement, Tuthmosis III became sole ruler with a prosperous and well-organised country behind him. Threats to the security of Egypt were already developing on the northern borders, and in a series of brilliant campaigns extending over twenty-two years he entirely removed the menace of invasion by winning and organising a rich empire in Palestine and Syria. At his death Egypt was firmly established as the premier world power.

THE GOLDEN AGE OF IMPERIAL EGYPT, 1436–1365 B.C.

Reigns of Amen-hetep II, 1436–1412; Tuthmosis IV, 1412–1402; Amen-hetep III, 1402–1364.

The imperial policy of Tuthmosis III was continued by his energetic son, Amen-hetep II, and by his grandson, Tuthmosis IV. When Amen-hetep III came to the throne, he inherited a tranquil and prosperous empire that stretched from the Euphrates in the north to Napata in the Sudan. In his reign, apart from an expedition to Nubia, no military enterprises were deemed necessary, and the King devoted himself to the pleasures of the chase and the arts of peace. The rise of Thebes as the main Residence city of Egypt advanced the fortunes of the city god Amen who attained a position of great wealth and influence. Other cults, however, faced with this challenge appear to have modernised their doctrines, including Ra of Heliopolis, a god who during the Old Kingdom had wielded great authority and who still enjoyed enormous prestige. The establishment of the Crown Prince's headquarters at Memphis, at least as early as the reign of Tuthmosis III, brought the heir-apparent under the influence of his priesthood. In the reign of Amen-hetep II the image of the sun's disc appears with a pair of arms—a forerunner of the more developed symbol of the Aten—a disc with rays ending in hands, some of which support the royal officiant or bring life to him, an intimate liaison being thus expressed in conformity with the thought of the age. Under Tuthmosis IV, who showed a special predilection for sun-worship, the new god, the Aten, made his full appearance; and by the time of Amen-hetep III, his cult had become a fashionable court religion.

THE AMARNA REVOLUTION, 1375–1358 B.C.

Reigns of Amen-hetep IV / Akhenaten, 1375–1358; Smenkh-ka-ra, 1361–1358.

In his later years, Amen-hetep III associated on the throne with him his eldest son, Amen-hetep IV, who soon changed his name to Akhenaten. The new co-regent and his queen Nefert-iti were fanatically devoted to the worship of Aten; and not content with building temples and shrines to him in most important towns, they founded a splendid new city for him at the modern El-Amarna, whither they removed their court soon after 1369 B.C. Here Akhenaten ruled for some years, devoting all his attention to the new faith, while the northern empire, already showing ugly cracks at his accession, began to crumble into an anarchy fomented by the rising power of the Hittite Kingdom.

In 1364, Amen-hetep III, a devout and liberal patron of Amen, died, and a moderating influence was removed. Akhenaten now proceeded ruthlessly against rival cults, especially that of Amen. At the same time, certain changes in the Aten doctrines were made in the direction of a more austere monotheism. But the tide of affairs was against Akhenaten. The unrest in the northern empire reduced the flow of valuable tribute and brought home a disgruntled soldiery. The closing of the temples and the confiscation of their revenues threw on to the market a mass of unemployed officials who could only live by exactions from the toiling peasantry. The forbidding of sacrifices and other rites must have removed much of the purpose from everyday activity and profoundly demoralised a devout people incapable of appreciating their

Pharaoh's quixotic ideas. Events during the end of the reign of Akhenaten are obscure, but must have been clouded by the death of his wife, her second daughter Meket-aten, and his mother Queen Tiy. He associated Smenkh-ka-ra, probably a younger brother, on the throne with him and married him to the next heiress, the Princess Mert-aten. Neither appears to have survived him and he was succeeded by another near relative the young Tut-ankh-aten.

THE AMARNA AFTERMATH, 1358–1315 B.C.

Reigns of Tut-ankh-aten/Tut-ankh-amen, 1358–1350; Ay, 1350–1346; Horemheb, 1346–1320.

Since the new King was a young boy of nine years, whose claim to the throne had been consolidated by the usual marriage to the next royal heiress, in this case the third daughter of Nefert-iti, we may presume that the government of the country was now largely in the hands of his advisers, chiefly the Vizier Ay and the Commander-in-Chief Horemheb. A return to the traditions of the reign of Amen-hetep III was immediately inaugurated. The King changed his name to Tut-ankh-amen and his wife adopted the name of Ankhes-en-amen. The cults of the old gods were restored, the worship of Aten was restricted, the temples were re-opened and the statues of the gods re-fashioned. Tut-ankh-amen, the last of his line, died at the age of eighteen, and his widow, after seeking unsuccessfully to obtain a Hittite prince as consort, married Ay, who thus secured the throne. After a brief reign, Ay, too, disappeared, and the way was open for the accession of Horemheb, who devoted his reign to restoring law and order to a country impoverished and demoralised as a result of the Amarna upheaval.

SUGGESTIONS FOR FURTHER READING

1. Background Study.

J. Capart and M. Werbrouck: *Thèbes*. Brussels, 1925.
W. C. Hayes: *The Scepter of Egypt, Part II*. Cambridge, Mass., 1959.
G. Steindorff and K. Seele: *When Egypt Ruled the East*, 2nd edn. (revised). Chicago, 1957.

2. Sculpture.

N. de G. Davies: *The Tomb of the Vizier Ramose*. London, 1941.
G. Legrain: *Statues et Statuettes de Rois et de Particuliers*. Tome 1, Cairo, 1906.
E. Naville: *The Temple of Deir el Bahari*. London, 1894–1908.
J. Vandier: *Manuel d'Archéologie Égyptienne, Tome III, La Statuaire*. Paris, 1958.
H. E. Winlock: *Excavations at Deir el-Bahri, 1911–1931*. New York, 1942.

3. Painting.

Nina de G. Davies and A. H. Gardiner: *The Tomb of Amenemhet*. London, 1915.
Nina de G. Davies and A. H. Gardiner: *Ancient Egyptian Paintings*. Chicago, 1937.
N. de G. Davies: *Paintings from the Tomb of Rekh-Mi-Re at Thebes*. New York, 1935.

4. The Amarna Period.

H. Carter and A. C. Mace: *The Tomb of Tut-ankh-amen*. London, 1923–33.
N. de G. Davies: *The Rock Tombs of El Amarna*. London, 1901–08.
H. Frankfort and Others: *The Mural Paintings of El-'Amarneh*. London, 1929.
J. D. S. Pendlebury: *Tell el-Amarna*. London, 1935.
W. M. F. Petrie: *Tell-el-Amarna*. London, 1894.
Various: *The City of Akhenaten*. London, 1923–51.

5. Articles.

C. Aldred: *The Beginning of the El-Amarnah Period* in JOURNAL OF EGYPTIAN ARCHÆOLOGY, Vol. 45, pp. 19–33.
C. Aldred: *The End of the El-Amarnah Period* in JOURNAL OF EGYPTIAN ARCHÆOLOGY, Vol. 43, pp. 30–42.
A. Fakhry: *A Note on the Tomb of Kheruef at Thebes* in ANNALES DU SERVICE DES ANTIQUITÉS DE L'EGYPTE, Tome XLII, pp. 450–508.

DESCRIPTIVE NOTES TO THE PLATES

The measurements given refer only to that part of the object which is illustrated.

The following abbreviations are used to denote the various archæological missions under whose auspices excavations have been conducted:

D.O.G., *Deutschen Orient-Gesellschaft,* Berlin.

E.E.F. (E.E.S.), *Egypt Exploration Fund,* later, *Society,* London.

M.M.A., *Egyptian Expedition of the Metropolitan Museum of Art,* New York.

S.A., *Service des Antiquités de l'Egypte,* Cairo.

1. STATUE OF AN UNKNOWN MAN. Painted limestone. Height 13½in. Excavated by Alexander Rhind at Thebes, 1857. Late XVIIth Dynasty. At Edinburgh (Reg. No. 1956. 140).

The unknown dignitary, wearing an elaborate collar and armlets, perches timidly on a stool with animal legs. The unusual freeing of the limbs from stone fillings should be observed. The surface has been eroded in places through the efflorescence of salts, giving the statuette the false appearance of having been coated with a skin of gesso before it was painted. There seems to be no reason for dating this object to any other age—the wasp waist and heavy hips are in the mannered tradition of the Second Intermediate Period and already appear in certain royal statuettes of the XIIIth Dynasty (cp. also No. 2). The elongated, slender proportions, the thrusting forward of a bird-like head, seen to advantage in a side view, are all characteristic of the archaic style prevalent at Thebes at the dawn of the XVIIIth Dynasty (cp. No. 3).

Photo: Courtesy, Royal Scottish Museum.

2. STATUE OF PRINCE AHMOSE. Hard limestone. Height 25 in. Probably originally acquired from Thebes about end of 19th Century. Late XVIIth Dynasty. At the Louvre, Paris (Reg. No. E. 15,692).

Prince Ahmose, a grandson of Queen Teti-sheri (see No. 3), died young. This statue of him is therefore almost certainly to be dated before the reign of his younger brother King Ahmose. The sharp cutting of the forms, the hard contours, crisp details and conventionalized portraiture, are in the academic tradition of the late XIth Dynasty and suggest that the sculptors of the period were already seeking inspiration in their own Theban past.

Photo: Courtesy, Sougez, Paris.

42

3. STATUE OF QUEEN TETI-SHERI.   Painted limestone. Height
14½ in. Acquired at Thebes, 1890. Reign of Ahmose. At London (Reg.
No. 22,558).

The Queen here represented as wearing the vulture head-dress
(the head of the bird which was probably of metal, is missing)
was the grandmother of King Ahmose. The limbs have not been freed
from stone supports, though the wings and pigtails of the head-dress
have been released from such fillings. The thrusting forward of the
head, the diffident 'archaic' expression and the slender forms appear
to be in the traditions of the period. This statuette, one of a pair, was
dedicated to the memory of the Queen by one of her retainers. It is
therefore most likely to have been made after her death, early in the
reign of her grandson.

Photo: Courtesy, Trustees of the British Museum.

4. STELA OF KING AHMOSE.   Limestone. 39 x 23 in. Excavated
by E.E.F. at Abydos, 1903. At Cairo (Cat. No. 34,002).

The upper part of this round-topped stela shows on the left, under
the winged disc, the king wearing the White Crown of Upper Egypt
and making an invocation to his grandmother before a table of
offerings. The scene is repeated with minor variations (the most
important of which is the substitution of the Double Crown of united
Egypt for the White Crown) on the right. The proportions, careful
drawing, sharp but shallow cutting and ordered symmetry are purely
in the conventions of the late XIth or early XIIth Dynasty. There is
nothing, in fact, to indicate a distinctive New Kingdom style.

Photo: Courtesy, Cairo Museum.

5. AXE-HEAD OF KING AHMOSE.   Cloisonné-work in gold,
electrum, carnelian, and glass pastes on a copper foundation. Height
3½ in. Excavated by Auguste Mariette at Thebes, 1859. At Cairo
(Cat. No. 52,645).

On this portion of one side of the head of a parade axe, inlaid
with electrum on a lapis lazuli paste background, the king is shown
wearing a war-helmet and smiting an Egyptian rebel. Below, the king
is described as beloved of Menthu, the war-god, who is represented as
a griffin with wings displayed, comb erect, and a scroll decoration on
its neck, differing in these respects from the normal Egyptian
hieracosphinx, and strongly suggesting Helladic influence, though the
inscription is purely Egyptian. This axe may therefore have been made
at Memphis, which was the great centre of the jewellery crafts and
where a number of Aegean and other foreign workmen had probably
come to settle.

Photo: Courtesy, Cairo Museum.

6. FLY OF QUEEN AH-HETEP. Gold. Height 3½ in. Excavated by Auguste Mariette at Thebes, 1859. Reign of Ahmose. At Cairo (Cat. No. 52,671).

This pendant, one of three on a simple gold chain, like the parade axe (No. 5), was found in the coffin of Queen Ah-hetep and appears to have been given to her by her son King Ahmose. The Order of the Golden Fly was a high military decoration, perhaps of Hyksos origin, awarded for valour on the field, and the somewhat incongruous appearance of such a badge among the parure of a queen is to be explained by the war-like character of the age and the influential part played in it by the royal women-folk. In contra-distinction to the elegant, rather spidery design on the axe-head, the gold flies show a massive stylisation, boldly determined by a simple metal-work technique, which seems to be more Egyptian than foreign, since it betrays the same genius for the conventionalisation of a subject into a powerful heraldic symbol as may also be seen in the pictographs of hieroglyphic writing.

Photo: Courtesy, Cairo Museum.

7. HEAD OF A SPHINX. Yellow limestone. Height 17 in. Excavated by E.E.F. at Abydos, 1900. Early XVIIIth Dynasty. At Edinburgh (Reg. No. 1900.212.10).

This sphinx, which was recovered by a trial dig in the area of the temple of Osiris at Abydos, may be dated on stylistic grounds to the early years of the Dynasty. The treatment of the eyes, with their pronounced canthi, and the musculature around the alae of the nose, show some affinity to similar features on a shawabti of King Ahmose in the British Museum. This specimen, in fact, may have come from the building dedicated to Ahmose by his son Amen-hetep I within the temple enclosure. The narrow seam along the inner edge of the lappets of the wig-cover is a legacy of the late Middle Kingdom, but goes out of fashion until the reign of Amen-hetep III when it is reintroduced (cp. Nos. 23, 53, 139).

Photo: Courtesy, Royal Scottish Museum.

8. BUST OF A QUEEN. Hard white marble. Height 11 in. Excavated by M.M.A. at Thebes, 1915. Early XVIIIth Dynasty. At New York (Reg. No. 16.10.224).

This fragment of the upper part of a seated statue of a queen wearing the vulture head-dress unfortunately lacks an inscription and cannot be identified with certainty. It must, however, represent one of the influential heiress queens of the period. The hard precise contours of eyes and lips are in the somewhat 'archaic' style of the earliest reigns of the Dynasty when the conventions of the Theban style of the XIth Dynasty were being revived. The subtle modelling around nose and lips should be compared with that in No. 7.

Photo: Courtesy, Metropolitan Museum of Art, New York.

9, 10. HEAD OF AN UNKNOWN KING. Green volcanic stone. Height 8¼ in. Excavated by S.A. at Karnak, 1928. Early XVIIIth Dynasty. At Cairo (Ent. No. 52,364).

The somewhat academic handling and stylised portraiture show the persistence and inspiration of the Middle Kingdom style of, for instance, the Karnak sculptures of Senusret I. There is already apparent, however, a certain delicacy in the forms which is quite foreign to the royal statuary of the Middle Kingdom. This head cannot be precisely ascribed to any particular king, though it is not likely to be later than the reign of Amen-hetep I. The raised eyebrows, and somewhat wide staring eyes with their sharp inner canthi are characteristic of the sculptures of the Dynasty until the appearance of a mature style in the later works of Hatshepsut (cp. Nos. 7, 15, 21).

Photos: Courtesy, Cairo Museum.

11. RELIEF OF KING AMEN-HETEP I, DETAIL. Limestone, traces of pigment. 9½ x 9½ in. Acquired, 1951. Provenance unknown, perhaps Thebes. At Edinburgh (Reg. No. 1951.132).

The pronounced aquiline features and the only hieroglyph in the inscription (not shown), make the identification of the king on this fragment as Amen-hetep I certain. The relief which is very shallow, like that of a coin, shows the king in his jubilee cloak wearing the Red Crown.

Photo: Courtesy, Royal Scottish Museum.

12. SECOND COFFIN OF QUEEN MERIT-AMEN. Cedar wood, faint traces of inlay and gilding. Height (to elbow) 45 in. Excavated by M.M.A. at Deir el-Bahri, 1929. Reign of Amen-hetep I. At Cairo (Ent. No. 53,140).

The tomb of Queen Merit-amen, the sister and wife of Amen-hetep I, was found in a sadly pillaged condition; and though the body of the Queen had been re-wrapped and re-buried in two of its original three coffins by the priest-kings of a later age, all jewellery and articles of worth were missing. Originally, the chevron-shaped depressions imitating the braiding of the wig, and the scale-like markings representing feathering on the upper part of the body and arms, would have been inlaid with dark blue glaze, and the rest of the woodwork covered with thick gold leaf engraved with a feather pattern (cp. Nos. 140, 153). Only the face and hands appear to have been left in the natural state of the wood, for they have been smoothed to a delicate skin-like finish. The eyes and brows have been re-inlaid by the later restorers. This coffin, a superb example of the joinery of the period, presents us with a masterpiece of conventional, idealised portraiture. The features are cast in the mould of those of the reigning monarch, Amen-hetep I (cp. No. 13), and bear little resemblance to Merit-amen herself, judging by the evidence of her well-preserved mummy.

Photo: Courtesy, Metropolitan Museum of Art, New York.

13. HEAD OF AMEN-HETEP I. Painted sandstone. Height 8 in. Excavated by M.M.A. at Deir el-Bahri, 1926. At New York (Reg. No. 26.3.304).

This fragment from an over-life-sized statue of the King in jubilee costume comes from a small brick temple at Deir el-Bahri. The characteristic aquiline nose of this Pharaoh is also known from several relief portraits (cp. No. 11).

Photo: Courtesy, Metropolitan Museum of Art, New York.

14–17. FOUR HEADS OF TUTHMOSIDE MONARCHS, in various stones, arranged here for purposes of comparison, showing differences in style and emphasis over a period of some forty years.

14. HEAD OF KING TUTHMOSIS I. Painted sandstone. Height 32 in. Excavated by S.A. at Karnak, 1903. Reign of Tuthmosis I. At Cairo (Cat. No. 42,051).

This head comes from a column in the form of an Osiride statue of the king. The bold treatment, which recalls that of the XIth Dynasty, is well suited to the colossal proportions of the sculpture and the nature of the stone.

Photo: Courtesy, Cairo Museum.

15. HEAD OF QUEEN HATSHEPSUT. Painted limestone. Height 49 in. Excavated by M.M.A. at Deir el-Bahri, 1925–27. At New York (Reg. No. 31.3.157).

This head is from one of the Osiride statues which the Queen erected against the pillars in the topmost porch of her great temple at Deir el-Bahri. The delicate modelling of this colossal feminine head is in the more developed style of her reign. Earlier work from the same site shows the broader handling and less naturalistic conception of the preceding reigns (cp. No. 14).

Photo: Metropolitan Museum of Art, New York.

16. HEAD OF A TUTHMOSIDE MONARCH. Black granite. Height 7½ in. Provenance unknown, acquired in London, 1950. In the collection of Mr. Albert Gallatin, New York. Perhaps reign of Hatshepsut.

Sculpture in black granite was not common on the Deir el-Bahri site and seems confined to certain half-size statues of Hatshepsut showing her as wearing the Pharaonic insignia but still as a woman. This less official aspect was probably the more permissible because such statues were apparently designed for installation in shrines where, unlike the large statuary in the temple, they would not be subjected to the vulgar gaze. This head which may be of Hatshepsut, may have been made about the same time as the black granite statues of Deir el-Bahri and by the same sculptors.

Photo: Courtesy, Brooklyn Museum, New York.

17. HEAD OF A TUTMOSIDE MONARCH. Green basalt. Height 8 in. Provenance unknown. Acquired, 1890. **Reign of Hatshepsut-Tuthmosis III.** At London (Reg. No. 986).

This head has been ascribed to Hatshepsut by some authorities, to Tuthmosis III by others. The weight of evidence seems slightly in favour of the former identification since there is a certain feminine delicacy in the front view of the face which is somewhat foreign to the wide-jawed portraits of the king (cp. No. 38). On the other hand the statue may have been made soon after the full accession of Tuthmosis III by a sculptor who was accustomed to working in the convention of Hatshepsut's portraits. This head already reveals the full flowering of the distinctive style of XVIIIth Dynasty sculpture, free from influences from earlier periods. The portraiture, though personal, is nevertheless idealised, and the masterly technique fully conveys a charming rather than a powerful conception of form. The heavy beard has been restored.

Photo: Courtesy, Trustees of the British Museum.

18-20. RELIEFS FROM THE MORTUARY TEMPLE OF QUEEN HATSHEPSUT at Deir el-Bahri. The illustrations have been taken from casts in the Royal Scottish Museum. (Reg. Nos. 1951.4, 1908.378, 1951.3).

18. RETINUE OF THE MONARCH. Limestone, traces of pigment. 37 x 20 in. *In situ* at Temple of Deir el-Bahri, Upper Court. Reign of Hatshepsut.

The reliefs of Hatshepsut at Deir el-Bahri show rather less of the inspiration of the XIIth Dynasty prototypes, and rather more of the spirit of the VIth Dynasty reliefs of Pepy II. More movement is conveyed, the outlines are softer, the draughtsmanship more fluid. The influence, however, may not have been direct, but may have come from the neighbouring XIth Dynasty temple of Menthu-hetep, so far as can be judged from the greatly ruined reliefs from that monument. This scene shows fan-bearers, servants and grooms in charge of cheetahs following behind the royal carrying-chair. The raised relief is very shallow and the drawing and cutting completely assured.

Photo: Courtesy, Royal Scottish Museum.

19. QUEEN AHMOSE. Limestone, traces of pigment. 10½ x 14 in. *In situ* at Temple of Deir el-Bahri, Birth Colonnade of Central Court. Reign of Hatshepsut.

The Queen is supported by two deities as she proceeds to the Birth Chamber. This detail will serve to show the degree of precision in the portraiture conveyed by careful drawing and cutting. The aquiline features of the Queen are shared by several members of her family (cp. Nos. 11, 13).

Photo: Courtesy, Royal Scottish Museum.

20. OFFERING-BEARERS. Limestone, traces of pigment. 16 x 20 in. *In situ* at Temple of Deir el-Bahri, Mortuary Chapel of Hatshepsut. Reign of Hatshepsut.

This relief follows the lines of Old Kingdom reliefs in its proportions and style, though the modelling is less thorough and is nearer to incised drawing.

Photo: Courtesy, Royal Scottish Museum.

21. STATUE OF QUEEN HATSHEPSUT. Red granite. Height 110½ in. Excavated at Deir el-Bahri, the head by Richard Lepsius in 1845, the body and other fragments by M.M.A. in 1926–28. At New York (Reg. No. 30.3.1).

This colossal granite statue, the head of which was acquired by exchange from the Berlin Museum, represents Hatshepsut as wearing the White Crown of Upper Egypt, and kneeling to present offerings to Amen-ra. It was originally erected with its fellows in the Upper Court, outside the Sanctuary of the temple at Deir el-Bahri. The massive simplified planes of this colossus is in keeping with the granular nature of the stone and the architectural role it played in the temple structure. It is a complete expression of the official sculpture of the dynasty. Though based upon Middle Kingdom models, it is more stylised and less dramatically realistic.

Photo: Courtesy, Metropolitan Museum of Art, New York.

22. STATUE OF QUEEN HATSHEPSUT. Hard white marble. Height 77 in. Excavated at Deir el-Bahri, body by Richard Lepsius in 1845, head and other fragments by M.M.A. in 1926–28. At New York (Reg. No. 29.3.2).

The body of this statue was formerly in Berlin until an exchange brought it to New York. It was probably designed for an important position, perhaps in the mortuary chapel, of the Queen's funerary temple at Deir el-Bahri. Though it represents Hatshepsut as a king in full Pharaonic costume, its delicate carving, elongated proportions, slender waist and rather full breasts give an idealisation of feminine grace which is yet in the Theban tradition (cp. Nos. 2, 3). This and other similar statues of the Queen may have been a contributory factor in giving to the sculpture of the dynasty a pronounced twist towards a tradition of femininity which develops throughout the period.

Photo: Courtesy, Metropolitan Museum of Art, New York.

23. SPHINX OF QUEEN HATSHEPSUT. Red granite. Height 65 in. Length 135 in. Excavated by M.M.A. at Deir el-Bahri, 1926–28. At New York (Reg. No. 31.3.166).

This sphinx, reconstructed as so many of the Deir el-Bahri statues from deliberately shattered fragments, was one of six from the Middle Court of the temple. It is a true sphinx, *i.e.* it shows the ruler as the sun-god Harmachis with the body of a lion and the head of a Pharaoh wearing the striped wig-cover (cp. No. 24). The massive stylisation is suited to the nature of the stone and the architectural purpose of these

monuments. The colossal sphinxes of Hatshepsut are clearly inspired by Middle Kingdom models from which they differ only in minor details and in the idealisation of the features of the monarch.
Photo: Courtesy, Metropolitan Museum of Art, New York.

24. SPHINX OF QUEEN HATSHEPSUT. Limestone. Height 24 in. Length 42 in. Excavated by M.M.A. at Deir el-Bahri, 1926–28. At New York (Reg. No. 31.3.94).

This restored statue, representing the Queen as a lion with the mask of a woman, is clearly in the tradition of such Middle Kingdom sphinxes as those from Tanis and Edfu. It is in soft limestone and was one of a pair 'which originally stood on the newel-posts of the lower staircase of the temple at Deir el-Bahri, flanking the entrance to the Middle Court. It is therefore probable that these sphinxes represent the two lion-gods with the features of the ruler, who are specially concerned with guarding thresholds. (cp. No. 151).
Photo: Courtesy, Metropolitan Museum of Art, New York.

25. STATUE OF QUEEN HATSHEPSUT. Red granite. Height 95 in. Excavated by M.M.A. at Deir el-Bahri, 1926–28. At Cairo (Ent. No. 52,458).

This statue, one of a pair, represents the Queen as a Pharaoh wearing the striped wig-cover, heavy beard and pleated kilt with ceremonial apron. It was probably set up in the vestibule before the upper gateway of the temple—a public place where the Queen could appear to her subjects in all the dignity of office. The pose and costume are obviously copied from Middle Kingdom models probably still standing at Karnak at this time. The enhancing of such details as the eyes with paint should be observed, as in most granite statuary such colouring has disappeared.
Photo: Courtesy, Cairo Museum.

26. STATUE OF KING TUTHMOSIS III. Red granite. Height 118 in. Excavated by Daninos Pasha at Medamud, near Thebes, 1914. At New York (Reg. No. 14.7.15).

A similar statue to the preceding, also probably set up before a temple doorway, and also in a somewhat coarse red granite which has prompted a summary treatment. The King wears the tall White Crown and in a side view a slight thrusting forward of the head (seen also in several statues of the period, e.g. B.M. No. 61) may be observed. This specimen presents a routine view of the subject in the official style.
Photo: Courtesy, Metropolitan Museum of Art, New York.

27. CRETAN TRIBUTE-BEARERS. Gouache on fine plaster over limestone. 22½ x 16¾ in. Tomb of Sen-en-mut No. 71 at Thebes. Reign of Hatshepsut. After the facsimile by Nina M. Davies.

The earlier tomb of Sen-en-mut appears to have been deliberately wrecked on his fall from power. This fragment with its lost or faded colours is nevertheless of value as one of the earliest and most accurate representations of a scene that was to become more popular in later reigns—the bringing of tribute by Minoan or Aegean people. The bearers are shown wearing the kilt with cod-piece and carrying vases of characteristic pattern. More than this, however, the artist has shown these envoys by means of the conventions which the Cretans themselves employed, suggesting that he was familiar with earlier and contemporary Cretan wall paintings.

From Davies and Gardiner: 'Ancient Egyptian Paintings,' Pl. XIV, by Courtesy of the Oriental Institute, Chicago.

28. PET DOG. Gouache on fine plaster over limestone. 11¼ x 8½ in. Tomb of Neb-amen No. 179 at Thebes. Reign of Hatshepsut. After the facsimile by Nina M. Davies.

The dog, wearing its collar, sits on a rush mat under its mistress's chair. The convention is certainly as old as the XIth Dynasty where a pet bitch is similarly represented on the sarcophagus of Queen Ashayet. The bold and assured caligraphy in the best Egyptian tradition is the basis of all Pharaonic painting and relief.

From Davies and Gardiner: 'Ancient Egyptian Paintings,' Pl. XV, by Courtesy of the Oriental Institute, Chicago.

29. MUSICIANS OF THE SCRIBE AMEN-EM-HET. Gouache on fine plaster over limestone. 20½ x 13¼ in. Tomb of Amen-em-het No. 82 at Thebes. Reign of Tuthmosis III. After the facsimile by Nina M. Davies.

A male lute-player and a female harpist and flautist are shown performing. The opening phrases of the songs they sing are inscribed before them. The stiff poses and the assemblage, rather than the grouping, of the figures are expressed by the same hard, precise drawing which is evident, for instance, in the reliefs on the sarcophagi of certain queens of the XIth Dynasty. This composition should be compared with the later version of a similar subject shown in No. 88.

From Davies and Gardiner: 'Ancient Egyptian Paintings,' Pl. XVII, by Courtesy of the Oriental Institute, Chicago.

30. MUSICIANS OF THE BUTLER WAH. Gouache on plaster over a mud-and-straw foundation. 17½ x 14¾ in. Tomb of Wah No. 22 at Thebes. Reign of Tuthmosis III. After the facsimile by Nina M. Davies.

The musicians dance as they play (cp. No. 88). A serving-maid offers a guest wine. All the adults have lumps of unguent on their heads adorned with lotus buds or flowers. The draughtsmanship is sure, but also stiff and prosaic: colouring is limited to plain washes of rather muddy colour with little interest in texture or quality. Conception and execution are in the severe economical style of the earlier half of the dynasty (cp. No. 29).

From Davies and Gardiner: 'Ancient Egyptian Paintings,' Pl. XXVI, by Courtesy of the Oriental Institute, Chicago.

31–34. FOUR STATUES, out of eleven known to exist of the same man, arranged here for purposes of comparison and showing variations on a group-subject consisting of a man holding a child. All four statues with their long dedicatory inscriptions were made by favour of the monarch to stand as votives in various temples at Thebes so that their owner might receive the benediction of the worshippers and a portion of the offerings. All four statues show the impact of an original mind upon the conventions of Egyptian statuary in seeking several different solutions of the problem of representing two human figures composed as a group.

31. STATUE OF THE STEWARD SEN-EN-MUT AND THE PRINCESS NEFRU-RA. Dark granite. Height 51 in. Excavated by S.A. at Karnak, 1904. Reign of Hatshepsut. At Cairo (Cat. No. 42,114).

A duplicate of this block statue was formerly in Berlin: another is in Cairo. Sen-en-mut is shown squatting, his mantle around him, holding his ward, the Princess Nefru-ra between his knees. It is evident that with this specimen the block statue of Middle Kingdom has become much more abstract and severe (cp. No. 48) There has been little attempt to model the forms of the body beneath the folds of the cloak, and the feet have been included in the wrappings and treated in the same stylised fashion. The body of the statue, in fact, has become a mere placard for the display of the dedicatory inscription. The heads of Sen-en-mut and the Princess have been carved in the same formalistic spirit and are no more than 'official' portraits. A similar statue in Cairo showing the Princess Merit-Amen with her tutor Beny-merit, is probably contemporary, or not many years older.

Photo: Courtesy, Cairo Museum.

32. STATUE OF THE STEWARD SEN-EN-MUT AND THE PRINCESS NEFRU-RA. Black granite. Height 24 in. Excavated by S.A. at Karnak, 1904. Reign of Hatshepsut. At Cairo (Cat. No. 42,116).

This statue presents the most successful of the various solutions of the problem. Sen-en-mut is shown wearing his temple-cloak, but there is evident in the pose, less desire on the part of the sculptor to produce a strongly abstract conception of the subject. Sen-en-mut squats on one leg in a somewhat unusual attitude but one already known from certain rare Middle Kingdom sculptures and from the large statue of his brother Sen-men, carved *in situ* from a large boulder in the Theban necropolis, who also nurses the Princess in an identical pose. The curve formed by the fall of the cloak over the lap provides an appropriate space in which the figure of the young Princess, represented conventionally as a child sucking her finger, naturally fits. The disposition of the large hands and feet is most happy and altogether a unity of subject and form is powerfully achieved. The age-old custom of representing the children of Egyptian kings as statuettes should be remarked. The subordinate figure of the Princess has its own supporting

back-pillar. It is clear that the aim of the sculptor here was to produce a composition of two statues rather than a statue of two persons composed as a group (cp. No. 34).
Photo: Courtesy, Cairo Museum.

33. STATUE OF THE STEWARD SEN-EN-MUT AND THE PRINCESS NEFRU-RA. Dark grey granite. Height 28 in. Acquired at Thebes, 1905. Reign of Hatshepsut. At London (Reg. No. 174).

Sen-en-mut holds in his lap the Princess, who as in the other statues is shown with the side-lock of childhood, her fore-finger in her mouth. This statue is the only one of the series which shows Sen-en-mut seated, and but for the bulge of the Princess's body under his cloak, would conform to the normal Middle Kingdom style, only the high polish and stylised portraiture betraying its New Kingdom date. It was doubtless installed by favour of Queen Hatshepsut in one of the temples at Thebes, perhaps in the chapel of Khonsu.
Photo: Courtesy, Trustees of the British Museum.

34. STATUE OF THE STEWARD SEN-EN-MUT AND THE PRINCESS NEFRU-RA. Black granite. Height 20¾ in. Acquired 1925, originally probably from the ruins of the temple of Amen at Thebes. Reign of Hatshepsut. At Chicago (Reg. No. 173,988).

This statue shows Sen-en-mut standing upright and stepping forward while holding the Princess in his arms. He wears a heavy wig, more common in the Middle Kingdom, which pushes his large ears outwards, and a temple cloak. The heiress-princess is here shown not as a statuette but as a person, for while she holds the sceptre of royalty in her left hand, she clasps the shoulder of her guardian with the other hand. From the front view, this pose produces an impossible anatomical distortion which, however, arises from the limitations that a purely cubic conception and technique of working impose. From a left-hand side-view of the subject, the pose does not appear so abnormal. It was only when the side-plane was worked into the frontal aspect that conflict arose which the sculptor, despite the originality and freshness of his vision, was unable to resolve, though he has to some extent cloaked the discord by a summary treatment of all the forms. The dedicatory inscription on the cloak already anticipates that tasteless smothering of temple statues with prayers and offering formulæ, which is characteristic of a later age although block statues during this dynasty had already become virtual placards.
Photo: Courtesy, Chicago Natural History Museum.

35. STATUE OF KING TUTHMOSIS III. Hard white marble. Height 15¼ in. Excavated by S.A. at Deir el-Medineh, Thebes, 1912. At Cairo (Cat. No. 43,507).

Like similar specimens showing the king kneeling to present two vases of wine or milk, this statue is probably an *ex-voto*. It is carved in an unusual stone, which however had been used earlier (cp. Nos. 8, 22).
Photo: Courtesy, Cairo Museum.

52

36. STATUE OF KING TUTHMOSIS III. Grey basalt. Height 79 in. Excavated by S.A. at Karnak, 1904-5. At Cairo (Cat. No. 42,053). See also No. 38.

The King, triumphant, wearing the White Crown, marches forward treading down the hereditary foes of Egypt represented as nine bows. This statue seems to reveal a new trend in XVIIIth Dynasty art. It recalls in the pose, dress and material, the classic striding sculptures of the Old Kingdom, for instance, the triads of Mykerinus; though if there is any connection, it is probably an indirect one from Middle Kingdom intermediaries which are known to have existed from a fragment excavated from the same site. The portraiture of the head is rather different from that of so many other statues of the king (cp. No. 26), and shows an attempt to catch a likeness. The rendering of the body musculature is in the same naturalistic style though more idealistically treated than in Old Kingdom prototypes. This statue must be regarded as one of the chief works of XVIIIth Dynasty sculpture and the master-hand responsible for it as contributing handsomely to the development of his craft during the period.
Photo: Courtesy, Cairo Museum.

37. STATUE OF THE VIZIER USER AND HIS WIFE. Black granite. Height 35 in. Excavated by S.A. at Karnak, 1904. Reign of Tuthmosis III. At Cairo (Cat. No. 42,118).

This temple dyad represents the vizier wearing his characteristic robe, striding forward with his wife Thuiu, their arms around each other. The marching pose is unusual for women, though not unknown, especially in group statuary. This specimen is a very fair example of the classical official sculpture of the dynasty. The portraits are highly stylised in the mould of the King's features, the expression urbane, and the slender proportions enhance the appearance of elegance and sophistication. A block statue of User in the Louvre shows the same style of portraiture.
Photo: Courtesy, Cairo Museum.

38. HEAD OF A STATUE OF KING TUTHMOSIS III. Detail of No. 36.

39. STATUE OF KING TUTHMOSIS III. Black granite. Height 32 in. approx. Former Drovetti Collection, 1824. Probably from Thebes. At Turin (Cat. No. 1376).

The upper part of the statue is shown here. It is a representative example of the work of the sculptors in black granite—technically very accomplished and idealistic rather than realistic in conception.
Photo: Courtesy, Museo Egizio, Turin.

40. STATUE OF THE SECOND PROPHET OF AMEN, AHMOSE, AND HIS MOTHER, BAKT-RA. Diorite. Height 45 in. Acquired 1890, ex-Sabatier Collection, originally from Thebes. Reign of Hatshepsut–Tuthmosis III. At Copenhagen (Reg. No. Aein 123).

The main influence in this double statue appears to be that of

53

Middle Kingdom prototypes as far as the pose, dress, coiffures, and summary forms are concerned. But the smiling expressions, careful finish, and smooth surfaces distinguish this statue very sharply from Middle Kingdom specimens.

Photo: Courtesy, Ny Carlsberg Glyptotek, Copenhagen.

41. STATUE OF THE STEWARD TEHUTI. Black granite. Height 33½ in. Excavated by S.A. at Karnak, 1900. Reign of Tuthmosis III. At Cairo (Cat. No. 42,123).

Tehuti, who was steward of Amen, and superintendent of the granaries of the god, kneels to present what was probably a statuette of a god or goddess or a triad, of which only the pedestal now remains. This statue is one of the earliest complete examples of a form of statue, which now becomes more common, showing an officiant kneeling to present the image of a god within a box-shaped shrine, and the first New Kingdom example of which had already been carved earlier for Sen-en-mut.

Photo: Courtesy, Cairo Museum.

42, 43. TWO STATUES showing the expression of a new idea which comes into fashion during the Dynasty—the representation of the deceased kneeling and raising his hands in a hymn of praise to the sun-god from his rising till his setting. Such statuettes were placed in niches high up in the tomb facade where they would catch the rays of the sun. See also No. 59.

42. STATUE OF THE SCRIBE ROY. Sandstone. Height 16 in. Acquired, ex-Rider-Haggard Collection in 1925. Reign of Tuthmosis I. At Norwich (Reg. No. 28.93.925).

This specimen shows an early form of the statue, which, however, was soon modified, since its strong diagonal forms offended Egyptian sensibility. The deceased kneels with his back to an inscribed stela and lifts his hands in adoraton. The filling between the forearms has been retained, and on this an abbreviated hymn to the sun-god has been inscribed.

Photo: Courtesy, Castle Museum, Norwich.

43. STATUE OF THE FAN-BEARER AND LIEUTENANT OF THE KING, PEH-SU-KHER. Black granite. Height 16 in. Acquired by purchase, 1910. Probably from Tomb No. 88 at Thebes. Reign of Tuthmosis III. At Edinburgh (Reg. No. 1910.75).

This specimen shows a more successful solution of the problem along typically Egyptian lines. The deceased kneels against a back-pillar and the stela is carved in front of his upraised hands as though supported by them. The cubic conception of form has thus been happily retained. The nearest parallel to such specimens in royal statuary is the king kneeling to present an offering to a god but no exact archetype can be traced in royal statuary.

Photo: Courtesy, Royal Scottish Museum.

44. WINE-CARRIERS OF THE VIZIER REKH-MI-RA. Gouache on a thin wash over limestone. 44 x 20 in. Tomb of Rekh-mi-ra No. 100 at Thebes. Reigns of Tuthmosis III—Amen-hetep II. After the facsimile by Charles K. Wilkinson.

The tomb of Rekh-mi-ra reveals the climax in the style of painting of the first part of the dynasty before new ideals had modified the artistic viewpoint. The draughtsmanship is still in the rather prim manner and tight handling of the earlier traditions, but greatly refined and self-assured. The artist, moreover, while accepting a hereditary technique, seems to have possessed original ideas on the composition of the scenes, perhaps under the encouragement of his patron who seems to have been concerned with leaving behind as much a memorial of the high culture and life of his times as a personal assurance of his own immortality. The scene shows men bearing jars of wine and bundles of papyrus stalks to the Treasury of Amen. The group is remarkable for the skilful designing and placing of the various masses, and for the variety of poses introduced. As if in contrast to the dominant rhythm of the pacing men bearing wine-jars on their shoulders, is the attitude of the bearers of burdens and the porters about to hoist up the wine-jars. Only in the drawing of the two men facing right is the old convention used of representing a group by means of overlapping parallel contours.

From Norman de Garis Davies: 'Paintings from the Tomb of Rekh-mi-re,' Pl. XV, by Courtesy of the Metropolitan Museum of Art, New York.

45. WATERCARRIERS OF THE VIZIER REKH-MI-RA. 10½ x 14 in. In the same tomb as No. 44. After the facsimile by Nina M. Davies.

The men are drawing water from a pond in order to make mud bricks. The composition illustrates the peculiar qualities of Egyptian design at all periods (cp. No. 160) being a combination of plan and elevation; of convention in the general design, and fresh observation in the details.

From Norman de Garis Davies: 'Paintings from the Tomb of Rekh-mi-re,' Pl. XVI, by Courtesy of the Metropolitan Museum of Art, New York.

46. BRICKMAKERS OF THE VIZIER REKH-MI-RA. 14 x 18 in. In the same tomb as No. 44. After the facsimile by Nina M. Davies.

From the same tomb as No. 45. The men are mixing mud with a hoe and carrying it off in pots to where the moulders are busy. The composition is cinematographic with its different 'frames,' the action unambiguous, the design constructed with sensitivity and restraint. It is the classical style of Egyptian painting at its most expert.

From Norman de Garis Davies: 'Paintings from the Tomb of Rekh-mi-re,' Pl. XVII, by Courtesy of the Metropolitan Museum of Art, New York.

47, 48. TWO STATUES of contemporary officials, with features cast in the mould of the royal portraits of their day. Both are in forms that originate in Middle Kingdom prototypes showing the sitter wrapped in a large temple-cloak. The treatment, however, is wholly in the urbane style of the XVIIIth Dynasty.

47. STATUE OF AHMOSE CALLED RURU. Dark grey basalt. Height 15 in. Probably from Coptos. Reign of Hatshepsut and Tuthmosis III. In a private collection in Great Britain.

Ahmose, who was Governor of the Coptite *nome* and Chief Prophet of the god Min of Coptos, is shown wearing a temple-cloak. In the inscription on the block seat he speaks of being shod thrice with a silver sandal in the presence of the courtiers under Hatshepsut (?), who also gave him a staff of silver and a dagger of gold. Tuthmosis III gave him a staff of silver and a dagger. The name of Hatshepsut (?) has been replaced in each case by that of Tuthmosis I.
Photo: Courtesy, the Owner.

48. STATUE OF THE PALACE OFFICIAL SEN-NEFER. Black granite. Height 31 in. From Thebes. Former Salt Collection, 1829. Reign of Tuthmosis III. At London (Reg. No. 48).

The owner is shown squatting with his cloak drawn around him, hands crossed on knees, so forming the classic block statue. The forms of the limbs beneath the cloak are subtly indicated, thus preserving a more naturalistic tradition in such statuary (cp. No. 31). Nevertheless the front surfaces of the statue and plinth have been treated as though they were walls for the display of the inscription.
Photo: Courtesy, Trustees of the British Museum.

49. STATUE OF KING AMEN-HETEP II AND MERTSEGER. Black granite. Height 49 in. From Karnak, perhaps originally from Deir el-Bahri. At Cairo (Ent. No. 39394).

During this Dynasty a number of notable animal sculptures appear (cp. No. 151). The most celebrated is the cow of Hathor from Deir el-Bahri, and also in the same style is this representation of the local snake goddess of Thebes, Mertseger, who was often regarded as another aspect of Hathor. The two statues have much in common : both show the goddess either as cow or snake wearing horns and disk and emerging from a papyrus thicket to protect Amen-hetep II who stands in front, hands flat on the apron of his kilt. Both statues refer to the myth whereby Isis-Hathor was supposed to have protected and sustained the infant Horus in the marshes of the Delta. All Pharaohs were regarded as incarnations of the young Horus, particularly at their advent. This statue is probably one of the earliest of the reign produced for the King's coronation ceremonies. Its dedication to Amen-ra like the mention of that god's name in the Hathor chapel at Deir el-Bahri, probably indicates that he is to be regarded as the father of the King, as Hathor was his mother.
Photo: Courtesy, Metropolitan Museum of Art, New York.

50. **STATUETTE OF THE ARCHITECT KHA.** Wood. Height 16 in. Excavated by Missione Archeologia Italiana at Deir el-Medineh, Thebes, in 1906. Probably reign of Amen-hetep II. At Turin.

It is a little odd that Kha, who held an influential position under three kings at least and received a fairly sumptuous burial, should have been content with so mediocre a tomb-statue as this, the descendant of such accompaniments to the burial in the Old and Middle Kingdoms. The assumption is that such statuettes had ceased to play any important part in the ritual of the dead, and it was only through some conservative idiosyncrasy that Kha provided himself with a shop-product. Certainly, a little later, in such an important burial as that of the parents of Queen Tiy, no such figures appear.

Photo: Courtesy, Museo Egizio, Turin.

51. **STATUE OF KING AMEN-HETEP II.** Green basalt. Height 23 in. Excavated by S.A. at Karnak, 1904. At Cairo (Cat. No. 42,077).

The king wears the *Khat* wig-cover and strides forward in a triumphant attitude (cp. No. 37). Like most of the work in this particular stone at all periods, the execution is masterly. There is, however, a certain suavity, a touch of over-refinement, that suggests that the style is beginning to lose momentum.

Photo: Courtesy, Cairo Museum.

52. **STATUE OF KING AMEN-HETEP II.** Grey granite. Height 47 in. Excavated by S.A. at Karnak, 1904. At Cairo (Cat. No. 42,073).

The king kneels to present an offering-table (cp. No. 41). The type of statue is known already from the representations of royal sculptures in the array of Coronation gifts depicted in certain tomb paintings of the period. This particular statue which must be dated early in the reign, belongs to the masterpieces of the of the first phase of XVIIIth Dynasty art, when sculpture had reached its maturity in the reign of Tuthmosis III. The style is an idealised naturalism expressed with great technical skill. No trace exists of the Middle Kingdom; with this, and the triumphal statue of Tuthmosis III (No. 36), the XVIIIth Dynasty style has come into its own.

Photo: Courtesy, Cairo Museum.

53. **STATUE OF KING AMEN-HETEP II.** Red granite. Height 60 in. Former Drovetti Collection, 1824. From Thebes. At Turin (Cat. No. 1375).

A comparison between this kneeling figure of a king making a libation and similar earlier specimens from the reign of Hatshepsut (cp. No. 21) will show that a softer, more naturalistic conception has replaced an architectural stylisation, with some loss of vigour in the process.

Photo: Courtesy, Museo Egizio, Turin.

54. **IBEX AND HUNTING DOG.** Gouache on plaster over mud-and-straw foundation. 24 x 22¾ in. Tomb of Ken-amen No. 93 at

Thebes. Reign of Amen-hetep II. After the facsimile by Nina M. Davies.

The decoration of the tomb of Ken-amen marks a turning-point in the development of painting during the XVIIIth Dynasty. The draughtsmanship is still confident, but in a more lyrical manner, and there is evident an interest in colour and texture as a means of expressing form, not as a mere adjunct to outline. This representation of an ibex brought to bay by a hound is part of a scene showing a hunt in the Eastern desert. The gullies and desert paths are shown as pebble-strewn ways cutting the folds of wasteland into islands against which the animals are represented. The stippling of the coat of the ibex has been achieved by the use of specially cut brushes and shows the artist's keen feeling for colour and texture as well as line. The interest in detail is meticulous without being niggling and is subordinated to assured drawing. Some later copyist has drawn red squaring lines over the figures of the two animals with a view to copying them.
From Davies and Gardiner: 'Ancient Egyptian Paintings,' Pl. XXX, by Courtesy of the Oriental Institute, Chicago.

55. CALF ASLEEP IN THE DESERT. 6 x 8 in. In same tomb as No. 54. After the facsimile by Nina M. Davies.

A further detail from the continuation of the hunting-scene shown in the previous plate. A calf hides in a fold of the ground. The drawing and brushwork are masterly. The artist also appears to have been an imaginative colourist not only in such details as the *pointillisme* of the desert paths, but in the choice of a sumptuous yellow for the background colour of the walls of the tomb in place of the usual white or grey.
From Davies and Gardiner: 'Ancient Egyptian Paintings,' Pl. XXXI, by Courtesy of the Oriental Institute, Chicago.

56. OFFERING-BEARER. Gouache on smooth, thick plaster, 18¾ x 28 in. Tomb of Zenro, No. 101 at Thebes. Reign of Amen-hetep II. After the facsimile by Nina M. Davies.

The bearer, the last of a procession, carries a bunch of lotus and a basket of grapes in one hand, and a bag of grapes and a dish of sweetmeats, which have attracted the attentions of two wasps, in the other hand. In front walks a prize bull-calf, garlanded on horns and neck. This painting derives from the classical style of the first half of the dynasty, but is more relaxed without losing anything of its assurance. The earlier discipline has not been forgotten, but the expression is more eloquent than terse. The painting is pure and fresh, but the pigments are laid on not symbolically according to convention, but in order to achieve a pleasing pattern of colour.
From Davies and Gardiner: 'Ancient Egyptian Paintings,' Pl. XXXVI, by Courtesy of the Oriental Institute, Chicago.

57–60. FOUR STATUETTES, dating to the middle reigns of the XVIIIth Dynasty, showing the variety of subject, pose and treatment.

57. STATUE OF THE LADY TA-NEFERT(?). Painted limestone. Height 8¼ in. Former Drovetti Collection, 1824. From Thebes. Probably mid-XVIIIth Dynasty. At Turin (Cat. No. 3094).

This statuette seems to mark a transition from the stiff, somewhat archaic statuettes of the beginning of the period (cp. No. 3) to the more relaxed and self-assured sculptures of the end of the Dynasty (cp. Nos. 142, 175). The costume is no longer traditional but that of the living.

Photo: Courtesy, Museo Egizio, Turin.

58. FIGURE OF THE GOD, BES. Ebony, copper and gilt. Height 6 in. Excavated by Alexander Rhind, probably from the 'Rhind Tomb' at Thebes, 1857. Reign of Amen-hetep II. At Edinburgh (Reg. No. 1956.113). Left arm and tongue restored.

This figure is from a casket first reconstructed in 1895 from fragments found in a box of debris from Rhind's excavations, and recently cleaned, repaired and restored. The figure of the household demi-god Bes is carved in heavy ebony, his mane and kilt being of gilded gesso; his spots are copper nail heads. It is probable that his feather crown may have been applied to the rim of the detachable lid, of which no trace remains. Bes grew in popular favour throughout the New Kingdom as a protective godling, and many representations of him exist from royal tomb furniture of this period : but it is doubtful if a synthesis of his leonine as well as his dwarfish character has been so well achieved as in this particular carving. Unlike the usual Egyptian conception of deity, he shows no assemblage of human and animal attributes, but a complete transfusion.

Photo: Courtesy, Royal Scottish Museum.

59. STATUE OF THE HIGH PRIEST OF AMEN, MERY-PTAH. Painted limestone. Height 12 in. Former Alnwick Collection (No. 508), originally acquired about 1816 from the unlocated tomb of Mery-ptah at Thebes. Later reign of Amen-hetep III. At Gulbenkian Museum of Oriental Art, Durham University.

This statuette is clearly related to similar specimens serving a specific mortuary purpose (see Nos. 42, 43), though the hands of the deceased appear to be holding the stela and not raised in praise. In statues where a person is represented as supporting a stela, however (e.g. the alabaster statuette of Akhenaten at Berlin, or Cairo, No. 42,121), the hands grip the edge of the tablet at the sides.

Photo: Courtesy, Dr. M. F. Laming Macadam, Durham.

60. STATUE OF A NUBIAN CAPTIVE. Bronze Height 5½ in. Former Abbott Collection, acquired at Sakkara some time between 1843 and 1852. Probably latter half of XVIIIth Dynasty. At Brooklyn (Reg. No. 37.267E).

This kneeling figure which seems to have come originally from a piece of furniture—perhaps a throne or canopy—shows a somewhat more plastic conception of form than is normal in Egyptian art,

perhaps because the statuette was modelled rather than carved, but more probably because the menial figure of a captive was being represented, allowing a certain amount of artistic licence.
Photo: Courtesy, Brooklyn Museum, New York.

61. PRODUCE OF THE DESERT. Gouache on plaster over mud-and-straw foundation. 17½ x 30¾ in. Tomb of Horemheb No. 78 at Thebes. Reign of Tuthmosis IV. After the facsimile by Nina M. Davies.

The military scribe Horemheb lived through several reigns but the context makes it clear that this particular scene was painted in the reign of Tuthmosis IV. The bearer carries a dish of ostrich eggs and feathers in one hand, and a desert hare in the other; an ibex accompanies him. The paintings in this tomb lack the precision and mastery of many contemporary painted scenes, but compensate for this lack with the verve and vigour of their drawing.
From Davies and Gardiner: 'Ancient Egyptian Paintings,' Pl. XXXVIII, by Courtesy of the Oriental Institute, Chicago.

62. NUBIAN DANCER. 8¾ x 14½ in. In the same tomb as No. 61. After the facsimile by Nina M. Davies.

One figure is shown among a group of Nubians who dance to the sound of the drum: The execution is summary, the form being built up as much by the scumbling of the brush as by the drawing of the outlines. It is probable that the decoration of this tomb, as that of some contemporary tombs, was in the hands of a group of artists who were not fully trained, or of the first rank, and lacked the mastery of more orthodox craftsmen. While they often reveal an incomplete or erratic control of their medium, in recompense they sometimes show a more original observation and 'deviation,' as this particular fragment testifies, where the very essence of the negro style of dancing, observed as a snap-shot, has been conveyed by fluid and inspired touches.
From Davies and Gardiner: 'Ancient Egyptian Paintings,' Pl. XL, by Courtesy of the Oriental Institute, Chicago.

63. THE CHIEF FOWLER PTAH-MOSE. 19½ x 8½ in. From same tomb as No. 61. After the facsimile by Nina M. Davies.

The old trapper kneels and with his hand to his mouth gives vent to the weird cry with which he decoys the birds within reach, or perhaps indicates his silence in the presence of superiors. The pelicans he has tamed preen themselves before him after the manner of their kind. The eggs are collected in pots with handfuls of grass to keep them safe and cool. The complete mastery displayed in this scene suggests that it was painted later, when the artist had perfected his somewhat impressionist style. The drawing of the pelicans and their trapper is observed with humour and executed with brilliant fluidity in the characteristic sketching-technique displayed in the paintings from this tomb.
From Davies and Gardiner: 'Ancient Egyptian Paintings,' Pl. XLI, by Courtesy of the Oriental Institute, Chicago.

64. STATUE OF KING AMEN-HETEP II(?). Black granite. Height 11½ in. Probably from Karnak. At New York (Reg. No. 44.4.68).

This fragment is the upper part of a seated statue of the King wearing the Blue Crown and holding the crook sceptre. Such a design appears to come into fashion in the reign of Tuthmosis III when the first examples appear in the paintings of royal statues in the tomb of Rekh-mi-ra. An actual example from this same reign is seen in a damaged usurped statue in Cairo (Cat. No. 42,192). The design of the Blue Crown on the specimen illustrated dates it to the period spanned by the latter years of Tuthmosis III to the earliest years of Amen-hetep III (cp. No. 78). The pyramidal top of the back-pillar and the idealised feminine features, among other things, suggest that the sitter is Amen-hetep II, though there is a chance that it could be Tuthmosis IV, his son.

Photo: Courtesy, Metropolitan Museum of Art, New York.

65. STATUE-HEAD OF KING AMEN-HETEP II (?). Black granite. Height 10¼ in. Said to be from Luxor, purchased 1913. At Baltimore (Reg. No. 22.229).

This head is from a similar statue to the foregoing and of the same date. The pointed back-pillar, like an obelisk, and the idealised portraiture suggest that this is also from a statue of Amen-hetep II, though of larger size than No. 64.

Photo: Courtesy, Walters Art Gallery, Baltimore.

66. STATUE OF KING TUTHMOSIS IV (?). Black granite. Excavated by M.M.A. at Thebes, 1915. At Cairo (Ent. No. 45330).

This upper part of a statue of a king was found among rubbish in the vicinity of Tomb No. 48 at Thebes, where it had evidently been dumped from elsewhere, perhaps from the funerary temple of Tuthmosis IV in the plain near-by. While it lacks any inscription that would indicate its owner, the high technical excellence and the bland idealistic portraiture characterise it fairly as a work of the XVIIIth Dynasty. The form of the wig-cover with its arched top and long unbordered lappets, the uraeus with coils above the hood, and the natural curve of the eyebrows place it in the period of the reigns of Amen-hetep II and Tuthmosis IV. The wide face with somewhat prominent cheek-bones and rather narrow eyes seems to be typical of the portraiture of Tuthmosis IV, whose statues, however, are too rare to form a reliable corpus for comparative purposes.

Photo: Courtesy, Metropolitan Museum of Art, New York.

67. STATUETTE OF KING TUTHMOSIS IV. Bronze. Height 5⅓ in. Formerly in the Acworth Collection, acquired 1946. At London (Reg. No. 64564).

The King kneels to make an offering of two libation vases to a god, a pose which is as old as the VIth Dynasty at least. His name is incised upon the belt-buckle. The outlines of the eyes and the brows are inlaid with silver. Very little metal sculpture made before the New Kingdom has survived in Egypt, probably because it was rare in any

case. During the Hyksos period, however, bronze became more common; and this alloy permitted statues and other objects to be cast by the lost-wax process with a degree of success that was not possible with the copper used formerly. (cp. No. 60).
Photo: Courtesy, Trustees of the British Museum.

68. STATUE OF THE MAYOR OF THEBES, SEN-NEFER, AND HIS FAMILYY. Black granite. Height 47 in. Excavated bv S.A. at Karnak, 1903. Reign of Amen-hetep II–Tuthmosis IV. At Cairo (Cat. No. 42,126).

This statue of a high dignitary of the period with his wife and daughter shows a fairly successful attempt to compose a group on normal Egyptian lines, whereby the cubic nature of the underlying forms has been preserved. Sen-nefer is shown wearing several gold collars of honour. While an intention towards producing a stylised official portrait is evident in this temple-statue, there is also apparent in the carving of the complacent peasant features, a realist characterisation which is outside the tradition of such sculpture. A short inscription on this statue states that it was made by Amen-mose and Zed-Khonsu, both of whom, besides being ordinary priests, were designers in the House of Gold of the temple of Amen.
Photo: Courtesy, Cairo Museum.

69. KING TUTHMOSIS IV AND HIS MOTHER, QUEEN TIO. Black granite. Height 43 in. Excavated by S.A. at Karnak, 1903. At Cairo (Cat. No. 42,080).

This is a later example of a type of double statue which in the XVIIIth Dynasty is figured among representations of royal statuary in wall-paintings at least as early as the reign of Tuthmosis III. This particular specimen shows the King with his mother, both wearing traditional dress, though the King's wig is of a fashion which he seems to have particularly affected. The workmanship is competent, but the forms are somewhat heavy. The figure of the king, who judging from his mummy appears to have been of slight physique, is carved in heroic proportions. The same heavy features that characterise the statue illustrated in No. 68 are evident in the figure of Queen Tio.
Photo: Courtesy, Cairo Museum.

70. YOUNG BULL GARLANDED FOR SACRIFICE. Gouache on plaster over mud-and-straw foundation. 17½ x 14¾ in. Tomb of an unknown man No. 226 at Thebes. Reign of Amen-hetep III. After the facsimile by Nina M. Davies.

The painting displays the full development of the mature style of the mid-XVIIIth Dynasty before its modification during the Amarna period. Expression of form is based upon sure calligraphic draughts-manship and patterns of sumptuous colour used as much for its own sake as for the needs of composition.
From Davies and Gardiner: 'Ancient Egyptian Paintings,' Pl. LIX, by Courtesy of the Oriental Institute, Chicago.

71. **LAST FAREWELL AT THE TOMB.** Gouache on plaster over mud-and-straw foundation. 11¼ x 8¾ in. Tomb of Neb-amen and Ipuky No. 181 at Thebes. Reign of Amen-hetep III. After the facsimile by Nina M. Davies.

The paintings in this tomb-chapel also display the full flowering of Egyptian artistic talent in pre-Amarna days. Drawing is precise yet unconfined and supremely confident; the colour is opulent and naturalistic rather than symbolic. In this representation, however, of the widow at the foot of her husband's coffin, there is evident an entirely new element—the expression of an emotion by means not only of posture but of facial contortion (cp. No. 150).

From Davies and Gardiner: 'Ancient Egyptian Paintings,' Pl. LXIV, by Courtesy of the Oriental Institute, Chicago.

72. **GUESTS AT A FEAST.** Gouache on white-washed plaster over mud-and-straw foundation. 12¼ x 9½ in. Tomb of Nakht No. 52 at Thebes. Reign of Tuthmosis IV(?). After the facsimile by Nina M. Davies.

A woman guest turns to her neighbour and encourages her to smell the flower-bud which she holds in her hand. All three women squat on a rush mat. They are in their gala finery and on their heads have cones of scented ointment which emit a fragrance as they melt and trickle down the hair and shawls, staining them yellow in the process. The artist has avoided the monotony of representing a row of persons in echelon, by incorporating in his composition an incident observed from life. The result is at once a more naturalistic view of the subject and a more coherent group.

From Norman de Garis Davies: 'The Tomb of Nakht,' Pl. XVII, by Courtesy of the Metropolitan Museum of Art, New York.

73. **HORSES AND MULES.** Gouache on white plaster over mud-and-straw foundation. 21¼ x 16½ in. From the unlocated tomb of Neb-amen at Thebes. In the British Museum. Reign of Tuthmosis IV or Amen-hetep III. After the facsimile by Nina M. Davies.

The drawing of the horses is spirited but conventional: the mules are more keenly observed, probably because as less common animals they had been subjected to careful and original observation. The contrast between the fiery horses which have to be held in check by the groom, and the mules peacefully eating from a tub and allowing their groom to doze on the step of the chariot, is the result of some artist's personal study from the life, and quickly becomes a conventional element in the iconography of the period (cp. No. 93).

From Davies and Gardiner: 'Ancient Egyptian Paintings,' Pl. LXVIII, by Courtesy of the Oriental Institute, Chicago.

74. **PART OF A RELIEF FROM THE BODY OF A CHARIOT.** Modelled in linen and gesso over wood. 12¾ in x 17 in. Excavated

F

by Theodore Davis and S.A. at Thebes, 1903. Reign of Tuthmosis IV. At Cairo (Cat. No. 46,097).

Part of the right side of the chariot-body showing the king in his chariot charging into a melée of Asiatics (cp. No. 150). These reliefs already show all the features of such scenes which appear on the temple walls of the succeeding dynasty. Some of the Asiatics are shown full-face, an innovation of the period which was copied on all similar representations.

From Carter and Newberry: 'The Tomb of Tuthmosis IV,' Fig. 4, by Courtesy of the Service des Antiquités, Cairo.

75. STATUETTE OF A GIRL PLAYING THE HARP. Limestone.
Height 5½ in. Provenance unknown, bought 1953. Probably reign of Amen-hetep III. At Edinburgh (Reg. No. 1953.321).

Statuettes of servants designed to wait upon the deceased disappear from burials during the late Middle Kingdom, though the concubine figure still lingers during the XVIIIth Dynasty. Probably this statuette of a young woman in her gala wig playing the Asiatic harp is to be put into such a category of objects. Although it is unfinished the carver has succeeded in noting and seizing a lively impression. The head turned full face to the spectator is unusual both in sculpture and drawing but is not inappropriate in the case of foreigners and menials (cp. Nos. 87, 150).

Photo: Courtesy, Royal Scottish Museum.

76. BOWL OF THE FAN-BEARER MAI-HER-PRA. Faience.
Diameter 5½ in. Excavated by S.A., Thebes, 1899. Reign of Amen-hetep II. At Cairo (Cat. No. 24,058).

This dish is a good example of a type of artefact that was manufactured with increasing skill throughout the dynasty. It has a deep cerulean blue glaze decorated with a pattern in violet-black showing fishes, lotus buds and leaves, and a gazelle browsing on a plant as she suckles her young—all within a denticulated border. The design consists of an assemblage of motives to fill a given space rather than the decoration of a circular area: but the whole is carried out with great verve and fluidity of line.

Photo: Courtesy, Cairo Museum.

77. MONKEY PLAYING WITH A BALL (?). Blue faience.
Height 2⅛ in. Acquired 1948, provenance unknown but reputed to be El-Amarna. Latter half of XVIIIth Dynasty. At Brooklyn (Reg. No. 48.181).

During the Dynasty, not only were such large specimens made in faience as the votive sceptre of Amen-hetep II now in the Victoria and Albert Museum, but small objects as well, requiring skill of a different sort, as is evident in this engaging figurine of an ape playing with a ball or fruit. The exact purpose of this specimen is conjectural: probably it is to be regarded purely as an object of vertu (cp. No. 103). A characteristic rococo feature of the later years of the Dynasty is a love of *singerie* which goes with a taste for such exotic and 'amusing'

subjects as Nubian children with their hair in tufts (cp. Nos. 162–163). Occasionally the two are combined as in the wooden figure in University College, London, of a negress carrying a tray supported by an ape, or in a faience fragment in Eton College Museum showing a negress carrying apes on her shoulders, or in a complete figurine in the Royal Scottish Museum showing a negress nursing three apes originally all wearing silver ear-and-nose-rings. The perforations in the ears of the Brooklyn specimen suggest that it too was once adorned with such rings.
Photo: Courtesy, Brooklyn Museum, New York.

78. STATUE-HEAD OF KING AMEN-HETEP III. Black basalt. Height 24 in. Acquired 1959, provenance unknown. At Brooklyn (Reg. No. 59.19).

The pattern of the Blue Crown shows that the statue from which this head comes must date to the earliest years of the reign, as is also suggested by the youthful chubby features of the king who was probably not more than twelve years old when he came to the throne. The thick arched eyebrows and the heavy outlines to the long almond eyes, are characteristic of the earlier portraits of the King as are the thick lips raised slightly at the corners in an aloof enigmatic smile.
Photo: Courtesy, Brooklyn Museum.

79. STATUE OF KING AMEN-HETEP III. Grey granite. Height 70 in. approx. In the Court of Ramesses II in the Temple of Luxor.

This statue is an almost complete standing specimen of over life-size, probably from the King's temple at Luxor, which has been usurped by Merenptah of the XIXth Dynasty. Companion seated statues originally from the same site are in New York. This specimen well illustrates the mature style of the reign, with the features rendered in a less abstract manner, though the eyebrows are still thick and arched, and the eyes heavily outlined. The detailed cutting and polishing of the hard stone are masterly. Worthy of note are such stylistic features as the thin inner border to the lappets of the wig-cover, the S-shaped coils of the uraeus and the double curve on the medial line of the lips.
Photo: Courtesy, Mr. Bernard V. Bothmer.

80. STATUETTE OF KING AMEN-HETEP III. Black serpentine. Height 9 in. Perhaps from Thebes. At New York (Reg. No. 30.8.74).

When complete, this statuette would have shown the King wearing the Blue Crown. The back-pillar is in the form of a *Djed*-column which suggests that the statuette was made to commemorate one of the later jubilees of the King, probably the third in his regnal year 37. In the dedication inscription, and in the titulary on the plinth, the name of the god Amen has been expunged. This statuette, like a smaller ebony specimen at Hildesheim and a stela in the British Museum, shows the King in his later years as a fat, bull-necked man, but in non-traditional garb with sandals, long fringed robe, and a cloak more commonly worn by women. It is in these features that we are most aware of the influence of the contemporary Amarna style. The corpulence of the old King has been realistically rendered in order to bring his physique into line with the pathological condition of his son and co-regent who often affected woman's garb and insisted on the exaggerated representation of his physical peculiarities. Such unflattering realism in a royal statue was unthinkable before the revolution in taste that Akhenaten personally introduced. The pose with hands clasped in front is un-Egyptian and may have been suggested by statues of foreign deities sent to the Egyptian Court by Asiatic kings.

Photo: Courtesy, Metropolitan Museum of Art, New York.

81. STATUE OF THE SECOND PROPHET OF AMEN, ONEN.
Black granite. Height 58 in. Former Drovetti Collection, 1824. From the Theban area. Reign of Amen-hetep III. At Turin (Cat. No. 1377).

Onen was a very influential dignitary of the age, besides being the brother of Queen Tiy, and could evidently command a master-sculptor for this imposing temple-statue. It is carved in a formal architectural style and its features, so far as can be judged from their somewhat battered condition, are carved after the physiognomy of the reigning king, his brother-in-law, whose portrait now becomes the ideal in the mould of which all loyal subjects have their own features cast (cp. No. 98).

Photo: Courtesy, Museo Egizio, Turin.

82. STATUETTE OF KING AMEN-HETEP III. Ebony over-laid on kilt with gesso, gilt; eyes inlaid with opaque glass. Height 10½ in. Acquired 1948, probably from Thebes. Last years of Amen-hetep III. At Brooklyn (Reg. No. 48.28).

This statuette was probably made as a gift to the King by a Court favourite on the occasion of his second or third jubilee (cp. No. 156).

Originally the left arm was held pendent at the side, and the right seems to have been clenched across the chest. The King, who must have been about fifty at the time, is represented as a remarkably young man in the idealising style of the orthodox Theban school, in contrast to the contemporary revolutionary style of Amarna. (cp. No. 80). Nevertheless, the slack rounded forms must be interpreted as the conventional representation of the excessive corpulence of the King.

Photo: Courtesy, Brooklyn Museum.

83, 84. HEAD OF QUEEN TIY. Green schistose stone. Height 3½ in. Excavated by E.E.F. at Sinai, 1904. Reign of Amen-hetep III. At Cairo (Ent. No. 38,257).

This little head, which was found in the ruins of the temple at Serabit el-Khadim, is a very precious document since the cartouche on the crown between the two uræi-cobras shows unequivocally that it is of Queen Tiy. The characteristic features of the Queen, with her pouting mouth, are here realistically portrayed, and differ considerably from the idealised features seen in certain reliefs and on the Medinet Habu colossus. This intimate portrait shows the same unsmiling, somewhat spiritualised, expression that characterises particularly the portraiture of the Amarna period, with which of course this head may be contemporary.

Photo: Courtesy, Cairo Museum.

85. HEAD OF QUEEN TIY. Limestone. 16 x 16¾ in. Acquired, originally from the tomb of Userhet No. 47 at Thebes, 1905. Reign of Amen-hetep III. At Brussels (Reg. No. E. 2157).

This fragment in low relief shows a more traditional portrait of the Queen, drawn with remarkable purity of line and sureness of cutting. Certain salient features are still faithfully reproduced, such as the down-turned fold in the corner of the mouth and the deeply channelled upper lip, but the expression is dignified and impassive. The quality of Egyptian official portrature at its best is here represented—a careful map of the features on an idealistic projection. The decoration of the band of the crown with the falcon of the sun-god Herakhty in place of the more usual vulture should be remarked.

Photo: Courtesy, Musées Royaux d'Art et d'Histoire, Brussels.

86. HEAD OF A QUEEN. Painted ebony. Height 4¼ in. Found in the ruins of a palace at Gurob in the Faiyum, 1905. Reign of Amen-hetep III. At the Berlin Museum (Reg. No. 21,834).

This wooden head is from a statuette which probably had a body of a different material. The head-dress has been altered in antiquity by covering it with a thick layer of linen and gesso decorated with blue beads, perhaps to simulate the conventional curls of a wig. This alteration completely concealed the gold and lapis lazuli ear-rings, one of which, however, is now exposed. The spike on the top of the head-dress was to recieve a crown which is missing, as are the two gold uræi-serpents from the brow. On account of its general resemblance to the inscribed head of Tiy (cp. Nos. 84, 85) this specimen has been identified as from a statue of that Queen. There are, however, certain differences, such as the double chin, heavily lidded eyes and pronounced lines from nose to the corners of the mouth, which seem to distinguish this wooden head from the Tiy portraits, and suggest that it represents a daughter of Tiy, probably Sit-Amen. The alterations to the wig may have been made when the Princess became a principal queen of Amen-hetep III. In profile, this head bears a close resemblance to the portrait-mask of Tut-ankh-amen (No. 158) who is usually taken to be a son or grandson of Queen Tiy.

Photo: Courtesy, Agyptische Abteilung, Staatlichen Museen, Berlin.

87. SINGERS AND DANCERS. Gouache on white plaster over mud-and-straw foundation. 27¾ x 12 in. From the same tomb as No. 73. In the British Museum. After the facsimile by Nina M. Davies.

This part of a larger scene of a feast in progress, showing the orchestra, should be compared with Nos. 29 and 30 to show what sophistication had made of a common theme. The delineation of the human features shown full face is unusual and seems to have been confined to the representation of menials and foreigners. The shading on the feet of the performers should also be noted. The spirited and varied design of the group of musicians is paralleled by the postures of the dancing girls whose pose and movements are more naturalistically rendered and artistically designed to meet the needs of the composition.

From Davies and Gardiner: 'Ancient Egyptian Paintings,' Pl. LXX, by Courtesy of the Oriental Institute, Chicago.

88. MUSICIANS. 15¾ x 19 in. In the same tomb as No. 72. After the facsimile by Launcelot Crane.

The flesh colours in this painting are deeper than is normal owing to the darkening of a varnish which was colourless when originally applied. In the composition of this group, the artist has shown the same desire to depict the character of an observed incident from life as he displayed in No. 72, and in achieving a more naturalistic conception, he has also obtained a more dramatic intensity. The action represented is the posturing of the nude lutist in the dance, as is shown by the placing of her feet and the twisting of her body, a *contraposto* which unifies the composition. That the artist was attempting to express some original observation is suggested by the more naturalistic rendering of the left breast in full face, instead of in profile which was the invariable convention.

From Norman de Garis Davies: 'The Tomb of Nakht,' Frontispiece, by Courtesy of the Metropolitan Museum of Art, New York.

89. CAT RETRIEVING. Gouache on white plaster over mud-and-straw foundation. 11¾ x 16 in. From the same tomb as No. 73. In the British Museum. After the facsimile by Nina M. Davies.

The tomb of Neb-amen contained some of the finest paintings in the mature style of the mid-XVIIIth Dynasty, evidently by a masterhand. This detail from a highly idealised scene of a bird hunt in the marshlands of the Delta, shows an equally ideal cat retrieving the birds that have fallen to his master's unerring throw-stick. The pose of the animal, the drawing and exquisite brushwork, are all equal to the artist's intention.

From Davies and Gardiner: 'Ancient Egyptian Paintings,' Pl. LXVI, by Courtesy of the Oriental Institute, Chicago.

90. FRAGMENTARY STATUE-HEAD OF A QUEEN. Yellow jasper. Height 5½ in. Perhaps from El-Amarna. Ex-Carnarvon Collection. Reign of Amen-hetep III. At New York (Reg. No. 26.7.1396).

During the Amarna period a number of composite statues were produced (cp. No. 121), and this fragment appears to be from such a specimen. The yellow colour of the jasper was the conventional colour in which the flesh of women was represented and indicates that the face is that of a princess or queen. The full lips and rounded features suggest Tiy. This lamentably mutilated fragment is all that survives of one of the supreme masterpieces of ancient art.

Photo: Courtesy, Metropolitan Museum of Art, New York.

91. HEAD OF A KING. Obsidian. Height 7 in. Excavated by S.A. at Karnak, 1905. XVIIIth Dynasty. At Cairo (Cat. No. 42,101).

The remains of at least two life-sized statues in obsidian were found at Karnak. They appear to have been composite statues (cp. Nos. 113, 121), perhaps the earliest examples of a kind of statuary which is peculiar to the XVIIIth Dynasty, and particularly to the reigns of Amen-hetep III and Akhenaten. The high technical accomplishment of this mask and its idealistic portraiture suggest the work of the former king. The colour of the stone may indicate that it is from the composite statue of a god, perhaps Amen-ra.

Photo: Courtesy, Cairo Museum.

92. HORSES AND MULES AT THE HARVESTING. Limestone. Tomb of Kha-em-het, No. 57 at Thebes. Reign of Amen-hetep III.

The decoration of the tomb-chapel at Kha-em-het in low relief, represents the high-water mark of the art of the XVIIIth Dynasty early in the co-regency of Amen-hetep III and his son (cp. Nos. 104–106). The work is remarkable for its varied subject matter, its lively handling and fine detail and finish. The strength of its composition, however, is largely that of its drawing, and in this it does not differ from contemporary tomb-painting (e.g. in tombs of Menna and Neb-amen) with its similar basis in the outline-drawing. The subject-matter, and indeed the iconography, may be the same, as this scene shows, where the rare representation of mules, already depicted in colour in a painting, is carried out in relief.

Photo: Courtesy, Metropolitan Museum of Art, New York.

93. MULES IN THE HARVEST FIELD. Limestone. Tomb of Kha-em-het, No. 57 at Thebes. Reign of Amen-hetep III.

Detail of the foregoing scene (cp. No. 73).

Photo: Courtesy, Metropolitan Museum of Art, New York.

94. RELIEF OF KING AMEN-HETEP III. Limestone. Width 43 in. Excavated by Flinders Petrie at Thebes, 1896. At Cairo (Cat. No. 34026).

Middle portion of a stela originally from the King's funerary temple but reused in the foundations of Merenptah's funerary temple (cp. No. 79). The scene shows the King mounted in his war-chariot riding triumphant over Asiatic foes on the left and African enemies on the right. The meticulous drawing and clean precise carving represent the classical art of the reign at its apogee.

Photo: Courtesy, Metropolitan Museum of Art, New York.

95. RELIEF OF A CHARIOTEER. Limestone. Height 9 in. Probably from a demolished temple at El-Amarna. At Brooklyn (Reg. No. 60.28).

This relief is illustrated here with No. 94 to show the contrast between the orthodox and the revolutionary styles of the period. The scene shows a groom or attendant, sandals slipped over his upper arm by their straps, racing his chariot to keep up with the royal retinue. The front view of one of the horse's heads is very unusual, though the pose now enters the repertoire and is sometimes found in subsequent Ramesside reliefs. The aquiline features of the charioteer, perhaps indicating an Asiatic, are typical of that freshness of vision that characterises much of Amarna art.

Photo: Courtesy, Brooklyn Museum.

96. STATUE OF THE ARCHITECT AMEN-HETEP, SON OF HAPU. Black granite. Height 51 in. Excavated by S.A. at Karnak, 1913. Reign of Amen-hetep III. At Cairo (Ent. No. 44,861).

Two statues of this most important functionary were found *in situ* in the Temple of Amen at Karnak, where they had been dedicated along with several others in the owner's lifetime. The pose of Amen-hetep, shown as a scribe seated cross-legged about to write on the papyrus roll spread out on his lap, harks back to the traditions of the Old Kingdom; but in the suavity of its forms, the elaborate wig, conventionalised rolls of fat on the upper torso and stylised portraiture, the old style is clearly worn with a difference. Its chief distinction, however, is in the facial expression which has none of the alert self-confidence of the Old Kingdom style of portraiture, but on the contrary is much more spiritualised and contemplative. The humility of the scribe with his head bowed in reverence before his god in fact expresses that new relationship between man and deity which was profoundly affecting the outlook of the age and was perhaps contemporaneously undergoing more violent expression in the Amarna sculptures (cp. No. 143).

Photo: Courtesy, Cairo Museum.

97. STATUE OF THE ARCHITECT AMEN-HETEP, SON OF HAPU. Grey granite. Height 56 in. Excavated by S.A. at Karnak, 1901. Reign of Amen-hetep III. At Cairo (Cat. No. 42,127).

This statue appears to be in a more severe style, harking back, perhaps as deliberate archaism, both in form and spirit to the Middle Kingdom, with its cloaked, volumetric austerity, its large ears, old-fashioned type of wig and realistic portraiture. Amen-hetep is represented as a sage, rich in years and wisdom, but the fracture of the nose at some time in its life, and the subsequent re-carving of the cheeks on either side to form depressions, have accentuated the appearance of wrinkled and shrunk old age.

Photo: Courtesy, Cairo Museum.

98. UPPER PART OF A STATUE OF AN UNKNOWN MAN. Limestone. Height 11½ in. Acquired, probably in Theban area, by Dr. Anthony, 1842. Reign of Amen-hetep III. At Birmingham (Reg. No. 69.96).

This statue-fragment, which has been described in its time by experts as representing a woman, is part of a dyad, the enclasping hand of the wife being still visible. It illustrates the refined, somewhat epicene, physiognomy typical in an age of luxury and sophistication. The portrait of the owner, in fact, appears to be cast in the broad smiling features of Amen-hetep III himself, and gives no hint of the new spirit of unction—the *mal de siècle* which was already abroad and troubling the minds and souls of men.

Photo: Courtesy, City Museum and Art Gallery, Birmingham.

99. STATUE-HEAD OF A MAN. Hard green stone. Height 4 in. Probably from Theban area. In the Collection of Mr. Albert Gallatin, New York. Reign of Amen-hetep III.

The man is shown wearing a curled wig and four necklaces of a type which in actuality was of gold and awarded by the King as a high decoration to favoured courtiers (cp. No. 112). The thick eyebrows, decoratively arched, and the fold of flesh on the upper eyelids are characteristic mannerisms of the reign (cp. No. 98). The high quality of the carving of the hard stone is also typical of the best craftsmanship of the reign.

Photo: Courtesy, the Owner.

100. PLAQUE. Carnelian. Length 2 in. Acquired at Luxor, 1912, ex-Carnarvon Collection. Later reign of Amen-hetep III. At New York (Reg. No. 26.7.1339).

This gem, shown here greatly enlarged so that the quality of its carving may be appreciated, is one of four known complete examples, and is from an armlet that perhaps originally belonged to Queen Tiy: the gold setting is modern. The hard stone has been most expertly and beautifully carved in great detail. The scene, which seems to commemorate a jubilee of Amen-hetep III, shows the King wearing the Blue Crown and holding sceptres, seated upon a throne with sides and back in the form of a protecting vulture. Tiy is enthroned beside him, and behind them is a personified life-symbol holding a flabellum. Before them stand two of their daughters shaking sistra and holding out notched palm branches signifying longevity.

Photo: Courtesy, Metropolitan Museum of Art, New York.

101. BOTTLE IN THE FORM OF A FISH. Coloured glass. Length 5 in. Excavated by E.E.S. in ruins of a house at El-Amarna, 1921. Reign of Akhenaten. At London (Reg. No. 55,193).

During the XVIIIth Dynasty, there was a great development in the technique of working glass and this craft reached an apogee in the reign of Akhenaten. Large vessels were made by winding threads of glass around a sandy core formed on the end of a pontil, and reheating the mass so that it could be worked, by rolling and combing into it while still plastic, glass threads of other colours so as to form wave and feathered patterns. Egyptian glass was nearly always made opaque and the richness and intensity of its colouring have rarely been surpassed. This bottle, in the form of a fish, is made from light-blue, dark-blue, yellow and white glass. Similar bottles in alabaster are known from the Middle Kingdom.

Photo: Courtesy, Trustees of the British Museum.

71

102. COSMETIC BOX IN THE FORM OF A GRASSHOPPER.
Painted ivory. Length 3½ in. Formerly in possession of Howard Carter. Collection of Mr. and Mrs. A. Bradley Martin on loan to Brooklyn Museum. Probably reign of Tut-ankh-amen. At New York.

This piece of *bijouterie*, more elegant than practical, which is believed to have come from an important tomb in Thebes dating to the end of the XVIIIth Dynasty, displays the rococo taste of the New Kingdom at its most exquisite. Though now incomplete, sufficient evidence remains to show that the object originally consisted of an ivory head and body to which were pivoted the ivory upper wings, skilfully carved with a camber to a feathered edge and turning on small ivory pegs. When opened these wings reveal a small cavity for containing the cosmetic. The under-wings are of wood; and the antennæ, of turquoise-blue glass which has largely disappeared: the legs are missing. The object was originally completed by a stand of some sort, doubtless in the form of a spray of flowers in wood, ivory, and glass. The body and wings of the insect are painted and varnished in black, brown, and red-brown, in a conventionalised representation of the natural colouring. Such an insect was probably chosen for the design of this cosmetic box because all over the Near East from earliest times, the locust has been a source of high-grade edible oil. It may well be that a very precious cosmetic was made from oil expressed from the locust or grasshopper, which suggested itself as the natural container for such an unguent. A similar specimen in wood at Cairo has a much larger cavity for holding the cosmetic.
Photo: Courtesy, Brooklyn Museum, New York.

103. GAZELLE.
Ivory, traces of light brown stain. Height 4 in. Acquired in Thebes, 1926. Ex-Carnarvon Collection. Probably reign of Tut-ankh-amen. At New York (Reg. No. 26.7.1292).

The horns and ears are missing; the desert plants on the base are carved in intaglio and filled in with thick paint. It is difficult to see what utilitarian function this trinket can have served, and it must be placed among those charming objects of vertu produced entirely for their 'artistic' appeal to the connoisseurs of the age.
Photo: Courtesy, Metropolitan Museum of Art, New York.

104. RELATIVES OF THE VIZIER RA-MOSE.
Limestone, traces of pigment. 91 x 56 in. Tomb of Ra-mose at Thebes, No. 55. Co-regency of Amen-hetep III and Akhenaten.

The remarkable purity of line and the subtle modelling in the graceful reliefs from this tomb, make an instant appeal. It is only on deeper analysis that the style is seen to be somewhat monotonous, with the bloom of a slight over-ripeness upon it, lacking the variety and vigour of reliefs in some contemporary tombs (cp. Nos. 92, 93). A peculiar mannerism is the representation of the eye in paint—a convention which also finds an equivalent expression in the statuary of Amarna (cp. Nos. 114, 121). This scene shows the parents and other relatives of Ra-mose seated to receive offerings.
Photo: Courtesy, D. Syme, Esq., Musselburgh.

105. OFFERING-BEARERS OF THE VIZIER RA-MOSE. Limestone. 31 x 42 in. From same tomb as No. 99. Co-regency of Amen-
hetep III and Akhenaten.
Two offering-bearers are shown from a row of three. The work is
a refined and assured rendering of the classic stereotyped designs.
Photo: Courtesy, Egypt Exploration Society, London.

106. MOURNERS OF THE VIZIER RA-MOSE. Gouache on thin
plaster over limestone. 20 x 27 in. In same tomb as No. 99. After the
facsimile by Nina M. Davies.
Ra-mose evidently died before his tomb was ready, and a wall
begun in relief was finished off in paint. The same master-hand responsible for the outlines of the reliefs seems to have drawn those of the
paintings. In this scene showing mourners, however, there is rather
more freedom in the sketchy lines of the design than in the carefully
carved contours of the reliefs. It reveals the main features of tomb
painting before the full impact of the Amarna revolution had made
itself felt. The new ideas have not been completely assimilated. The
group shows a certain variety of gesture, pose and expression within
a greater unity, but there are still traditional elements as in the five
mourners on the right incongruously jostling their individual com-
panions, with their identity of posture represented by the old device
of overlapping parallel contours.
*From Davies and Gardiner: 'Ancient Egyptian Paintings,' Pl. LXXII,
by Courtesy of the Oriental Institute, Chicago.*

107-109. STATUES OF KING AKHENATEN. Painted sandstone.
Original height, over 13 feet. Excavated by S.A. at Karnak, 1926-32.
Co-regency of Amen-hetep III and Akhenaten. At Cairo (Ent. Nos.
49,528, 55,938, 49,529).
Excavations at Karnak have brought to light the existence of a
temple to the Aten erected in the early years of Akhenaten's co-
regency. Only the ruins of the N.W. angle of a large peristyle court
can now be traced with the remains of some thirty square pillars
against which were placed colossal statues of the kind illustrated. Each
shows the King standing erect, bearded and wearing a crown which
differs from those worn by companion statues, and holding the crook
and 'flail' sceptres of authority. Some examples show him clothed in
a kilt and apron (No. 107), one as presumably naked and sexless since
no attachment for an apron in metal or other material is visible (No.
108). The King wears bracelets and pectorals bearing the early names
of his god, the Aten, but of these only the raised bezels now remain,
the painted straps have disappeared.
Such statues of kings standing against pillars as part of an architectural composition are known from earliest times, but almost all,
and certainly the XVIIIth Dynasty examples, show the king in jubilee-
costume or in mummy-wrappings as a resurrected immortal, assimilated to Osiris the eternal king of the Underworld. Where the Akhenaten,
colossi are unusual is that they show the king as a vital terrestrial

ruler in the costume of the living—an innovation which appears to have been followed by later kings as at Medinet Habu and Abu Simbel. If, in making such colossi, Akhenaten was challenging comparison with the Osiride pillars in the temples of his forefathers, we may assume perhaps that he has chosen to represent himself as assimilated to his god, the Aten, a supposition which is supported by the inscribing of the names of the Aten on all the pectorals and ornaments in place of his own name which would be the more normal practice. This attempt to represent the ruler as imbued with the divinity of the Aten, may help to explain the extraordinary expressionist distortion of form in these sculptures, unparalleled in any art of the Ancient World. The long face, hanging jaw, gaunt collar bones, prominent hips and spindle-shanks of the King have all been exaggerated to such an extent as to lose their natural significance and to take on a new super-human symbolism—a stigmata.

Photos: Courtesy, Cairo Museum.

110. **THE ROYAL FAMILY WORSHIPPING THE ATEN.** Limestone. 19 x 20 in. Excavated by S.A. at Royal Tomb, El-Amarna, 1891–2. About 7th Year of Reign of Akhenaten. At Cairo (Cat. No. 54,517).

This fragment in sunk relief, which is important as showing the standard of workmanship of a sculptor employed on a royal commission, illustrates very well the peculiar mannerism of the early Amarna style. The elongated skull of the King is further exaggerated by the form of the crown and by the long crooked neck on which it is placed; the thickness of the hips is accentuated by the slender waist and the attenuated shape of the legs. While there is thus no attempt to render a naturalistic view of the subject, such details as the jugular arteries, the navel, ears, nostrils and lips have been over-emphasised. Similar distortions are apparent in the figures of Queen Nefert-iti and the Princesses, though to a lesser extent. The scene is thus rendered with an intensity and excess that would be caricature if the purpose was not quite different—to create a new religious symbolism recalling little of the past. The Aten is represented as the sun's disc from which radiate beams ending in hands that embrace the King and Queen, hold the breath of life to their nostrils, and accept the flower-offerings on the altars. The Princess Mert-aten shakes a sistrum behind her mother, and holds by the hand her sister Maket-aten who died young.

Photo: Courtesy, Cairo Museum.

111. **AN OLD COURTIER.** Limestone. $12\frac{1}{4}$ x $5\frac{1}{2}$ in. Acquired ex-Brummer Collection, 1947, originally from Memphis. Reign of Akhenaten(?). At Brooklyn (Reg. No. 47.120.1).

This relief shows an old courtier, wearing a wig of a kind represented in No. 171). His emaciated condition, shrivelled arms, fallen-in mouth, wrinkled visage and prominent collar-bones, have been ruthlessly portrayed. The portraiture is evidently individualised. The

old official appears to be near a canopy supported on light columns, one of which is visible in this fragment. His hand is held out in a gesture of adjuration, suggesting that he is receiving a delegation of sorts. If he were in the presence of the King, it is more likely that his back would be humbly bent in the true Amarna fashion.
Photo: Courtesy, Brooklyn Museum.

112. THE FAN-BEARER AND MASTER OF THE HORSE, AY, AND HIS WIFE TIY. Limestone. 17 x 10⅛ in. From the tomb of Ay at El-Amarna. Earlier reign of Akhenaten. At Cairo (Temp. No. 10.11.26.1).

Ay and his wife in festal attire, with cones of fragment unguent on their heads and fillets binding their hair, stand before the palace ' Window of Appearances' to receive the gifts which a generous Royal Family are showering upon their favourites. Around the necks of this pair hang the heavy gold necklaces of honour; and Ay is about to receive an elaborate faience collar. The work is characteristic of early Amarna relief at its best, skilful craftsmen having been employed evidently upon the large tomb of this important functionary. The draughtsmanship is assured and lacks the exaggeration and even frank ineptitude of some earlier work at El-Amarna. The portraiture within the limits of the convention is careful and individualised (cp. No. 173).
From Norman de Garis Davies: ' Rock Tombs of El Amarna' VI, Pl. XXXVIII, by Courtesy of the Egypt Exploration Society, London.

113. HEAD OF A PRINCESS. Brown sandstone. Height 8¼ in. Excavated by D.O.G. in ruins of a sculptor's studio at El-Amarna (1911–13). Later reign of Akhenaten. At the Berlin Museum (Reg. No. 21,223).

This head was originally designed as part of a composite statue, the eyes and eyebrows were to be inlaid, and the body was probably to have been of white limestone.
Photo: Courtesy, Agyptische Abteilung, Staatlichen Museen, Berlin.

114. HEAD OF A PRINCESS. Yellow quartzite. Height 8¼ in. Excavated by D.O.G. at El-Amarna, 1911–13. Reign of Akhenaten. At Cairo (Ent. No. 44,869).

This head is also part of a composite statue. It has the same exaggerated shape of the skull as characterises so many of the sculptures of the earlier part of the reign; but the surfaces are carefully finished and the modelling shows some keen observation of facial anatomy. In profile, the head bears a close resemblance to the high reliefs of the goddesses at the corners of the sarcophagus of Tut-ankh-amen (cp. No. 161). It may, therefore, represent the Princess Ankhes-en-pa-aten. The eyes are not inlaid, but are carved without any indication of a lower lid: the details were to be supplied in paint.
Photo: Courtesy, Cairo Museum.

115. **TWO YOUNG DAUGHTERS OF QUEEN NEFERTI-ITI.**
Gouache on thin plaster over mud and mud-brick. 14 x 11¾ in. Excavated by Flinders Petrie in the ruins of a palace at El-Amarna, 1891. Reign of Akhenaten. At Oxford (Reg. No. 1893.1). Reign of Akhenaten. At Oxford (Reg. No. 1893.1). After the facsimile by Nina M. Davies.

This fragment which comes from a larger scene showing the royal children gathered around their seated parents, is one of the rare examples of secular (as distinct from tomb) painting to have survived from Ancient Egypt. The two little girls turn to one another in contrasting postures (cp. No. 72), which give not only a unity to the group but an appearance of naturalism. Despite the mannerisms of the Amarna style—inflated thighs, over-slender lower legs, elongated skulls—and the still dominant conventions of Egyptian drawing—four right hands—the artist has successfully caught a mood and a dramatic moment as the two infants disregard the rest of the family in order to play with each other. This fragment makes us regret the loss of the whole scene which would have shown us a most striking 'conversation-piece.'

From Davies and Gardiner: ' Ancient Egyptian Paintings,' Pl. LXXIV, by Courtesy of the Oriental Institute, Chicago.

116. **THE ROYAL FAMILY.** Limestone. 15¼ x 12¼ in. Acquired from El-Amarna area about 1891. Earlier years of reign of Akhenaten. At the Berlin Museum (Reg. No. 14,145).

This stela, probably from a private chapel, gives a more complete idea of the Amarna conversation-piece. It is in the earlier and more *outré* style of the 'new art' of the period, and clearly displays the interest of the artist in composing a unified group, held together not by the action in which they are co-operating but by a psychological relationship. The King and Queen sit on opposite sides facing each other, according to traditional ideas of symmetry, but their poses and expressions are different. The two groups are brought together dramatically, by the linking pose of the princess on her mother's knee, who looks up at her as she points to the pair on the opposite side; and artistically, by the symbol of the all-pervading Aten with its beneficent rays mounting up to the supreme focal point of the disc itself.

Photo: Courtesy, Agyptische Abteilung, Staatlichen Museen,. Berlin.

117. **PAIR STATUE OF AKHENATEN AND NEFERT-ITI.** Painted limestone. Height 9 in. Acquired ex-Curtis Collection, 1938, probably originally from El-Amarna. Later reign of Akhenaten. At the Louvre (Reg. No. E. 15,593).

This little dyad is important, for apart from its intrinsic merits, the names of the persons represented are painted on the back, making the identification a matter of certainty. The inscriptions give the late forms of the names of the Aten, dating the specimen to after the ninth year of the reign, as the style also suggests. Akhenaten, wearing a kilt, sandals, Blue Crown and elaborate collar, leads his wife by the

hand. She is dressed in a pleated garment tied under the breasts by a
long red girdle. She too wears sandals, a floral collar and her
characteristic Blue Crown. Her large ear-plugs should be remarked,
as these appear on other representations presumed to be of her (cp.
Nos. 124, 125). Akhenaten in this statue is shown more as a normal
person, apart from the rather full hips which are also characteristic
of some of his father's statues (cp. Nos. 80, 82).
Photo: Courtesy, Sougez, Paris.

118. STATUE OF A KING KISSING A PRINCESS. Limestone.
Height 16½in. Excavated by D.O.G. in ruins of a studio at El-Amarna,
1911–13. Later reign of Akhenaten. At Cairo (Ent. No. 44,866).

This unfinished statuette shows an unusual group, though the pose
had already existed for several reigns in paintings representing young
kings in the laps of their nurses, and earlier still in statues of goddesses
suckling infant kings. The artist, so far as one can judge, has solved
the problem of representing two individuals in a group more successfully than an earlier attempt (cp. No. 34), though he has not departed
from normal Egyptian conventions.
Photo: Courtesy, Cairo Museum.

119. UNFINISHED HEAD OF A QUEEN. Quartzite. Height 13 in.
Excavated by E.E.S. at El-Amarna, 1932–33. Reign of Akhenaten. At
Cairo (Ent. No. 59,286).

The queen represented is probably Nefert-iti. The head is part of a
composite statue, having a tang at the base for insertion into a body
of other material. A close-fitting wig of faience or stone, covering the
ears, was meant to be attached to the upper part. The sculptor's
guide-lines are still in evidence, but the head is not far from com-
pletion: the eyes show the Amarna convention of representing only the
upper lid in relief. The fine sensitive modelling of the underlying
structure of the face is in the naturalistic style of the later half of the
period.
Photo: Courtesy, Egypt Exploration Society, London.

120. PORTRAIT BUST OF QUEEN NEFERT-ITI. Painted limestone. Height 23 in. Excavated by D.O.G. at El-Amarna, 1912–13.
Later reign of Akhenaten. At the Berlin Museum (Reg. No. 21,300).

This bust, the most publicised of all Egyptian antiquities, was found
by the German excavators in the ruins of a sculptor's studio and seems
almost certainly to represent Queen Nefert-iti wearing a head-dress
which she seems to have made peculiarly her own, consisting as it
does of a tall conical cap encircled by a band and streamers carrying
the uræus-cobras. Such a crown may have been designed to match the
Blue Crown affected by her husband, though it, or something like it,
also appears on female sphinxes of a somewhat un-Egyptian type. The
sculptor has elegantly elongated the neck of the Queen to balance this
tall cap. The bust proper is extremely rare in Egyptian sculpture, and

such examples as exist appear to have been made for the performance of certain burial rites. This particular specimen, however, seems to have served as a model for the guidance of lesser sculptors in the studio, and shows in its refined modelling and confident design the work of a mature master of the Amarna school of sculpture.

Photo: Courtesy, Agyptische Abteilung, Staatlichen Museen, Berlin.

121. HEAD OF QUEEN NEFERT-ITI(?). Brown sandstone. Height 8½ in. Excavated by D.O.G. in ruins of a sculptor's studio at El-Amarna, 1911–13. Later reign of Akhenaten. At the Berlin Museum (Reg. No. 21.220).

This head is from a composite statue in which the various stones would suggest by their different colours the materials and forms they were supposed to represent. Thus this head in conventional flesh-tone would have been sunk into a clothed body of white limestone and have received a crown in bluish granite or faience to fit on the upper part of the head (cp. Nos. 119, 127–129). This portrait head which probably gives an idealised representation of Queen Nefert-iti is most ably carved in a granular stone and is incomplete, though the sculptor has coloured in the lips, nostrils, and borders of the eyes as a guide for the final modelling and polishing.

Photo: Courtesy, Agyptische Abteilung, Staatlichen Museen, Berlin.

122. HEAD OF A PRINCESS. Painted limestone. Height 6 in. Acquired in 1937, originally perhaps from El-Amarna. Reign of Akhenaten(?). At the Louvre (Reg. No. E. 14,715).

This head has been attributed to one of the daughters of Akhenaten, though it could equally well be of a daughter of Amen-hetep III, judging by the representation of his female offspring in the tomb of Kheruef at Thebes. Instead of the shaven poll of the royal princesses, this specimen shows the owner wearing a wig and side-lock fashionable from the later years of Amen-hetep III (cp. No. 154). Enough of the dress also remains to show that the princess is wearing an elaborate festal collar and a pleated garment.

Photo: Courtesy, Sougez, Paris.

123. HEAD OF A ROYAL OFFICIAL. Plaster. Height 10¾ in. Excavated by D.O.G. in the ruins of a sculptor's studio at El-Amarna, 1911–13. Later reign of Akhenaten. At the Berlin Museum (Reg. No. 21,350).

This unfinished mask, as the symmetry shows, especially around the eyebrows and in the corrugations of the forehead, is not a cast from the life, but more probably from a modelled study in clay or wax. The plaster is in process of being worked into an acceptable likeness of the sitter. The upper lip has been marked with red paint, doubtless by the master sculptor to indicate an area requiring further carving. This particular head has been claimed as a likeness of Ay (cp. No. 174), but in the absence of an inscription, such identifications on portraiture alone are apt to be hazardous.

Photo: Courtesy, Agyptische Abteilung, Staatlichen Museen, Berlin.

124, 125. STATUE OF QUEEN NEFERT-ITI(?). Limestone, traces of pigment. Height 16 in. Excavated by D.O.G. at Amarna, 1911–13. Later reign of Akhenaten. At the Berlin Museum (Reg. No. 21,263).

This remarkable statuette, from the ruins of a sculptor's studio, shows a queen, who may well be Nefert-iti, with all the naturalistic fidelity of the period. There is little of the Amarna mannerism evident, and such traditional Egyptian features as the back-pillar seem architectonically necessary. The sad expression is one of inward suffering in the style of the period, but while there is an absence of idealism in the sensitive nervous modelling of the face, neck and breast (cp. No. 120), there is also none of the exaggeration verging on caricature of the earlier phase : even the heavy hips and paunch may well represent that pregnancy from which the Queen can seldom have been free. She is shown with the close-fitting cap that she is sometimes represented as wearing on reliefs (cp. No. 131), and large ear-studs. She is clothed in a close-fitting dress that reveals her form as she steps forward. This little statue which was broken and mended in antiquity, must be regarded as one of the original masterpieces of the dynasty, owing nothing to what had been created before.

Photos: Courtesy, Agyptische Abteilung, Staatlichen Museen, Berlin.

126. STATUE OF KING AKHENATEN(?). Yellow steatite. Height 6 in. Detail, showing side view of the head of the statue illustrated in Plate No. 134.

Photo: Courtesy, Archives Photographiques, Paris.

127. HEAD OF KING SMENKH-KA-RA(?). Painted limestone. Height 8¼ in. Excavated by D.O.G. in the ruins of a sculptor's studio at El-Amarna, 1911–13. Later reign of Akhenaten. At the Berlin Museum (Reg. No. 20,496).

The sculptor's studio at El-Amarna contained a number of sculptures and casts of the ruling family and their followers carved and modelled in the last years of the reign before the abandonment of the city. There may also have been representations of such actors in the Amarna drama as Amen-hetep III and Tiy, who were both dead before the co-regency of Akhenaten and Smenkh-ka-ra. It should therefore be possible to identify sculptures of Akhenaten, Nefert-iti, Mert-aten, Smenkh-ka-ra, Ankhes-en-pa-aten, Tut-ankh-aten and others. The difficulty is that apart from the conventions of portraiture, all these closely related rulers bore a strong family resemblance to each other, which makes the work of identification, in the absence of inscriptions, extremely hazardous. The youthful features of this particular head are softer and more idealised than those of Akhenaten, and the formation of the lips and chin is rather different, suggesting that the head is meant to represent Smenkh-ka-ra, of whom no inscribed statue exists.

Photo: Courtesy, Agyptische Abteilung, Staatlichen Museen, Berlin.

128. HEAD OF KING AKHENATEN(?). Plaster Height 12 in. Excavated by D.O.G. at El-Amarna, 1911–13. Later reign of Akhenaten. At the Berlin Museum (Reg. No. 21,348).

This is a plaster cast evidently from a composite statue of the King wearing the War Crown, the fillet of which may be seen on the brow and above the ears. The features seem to represent Akhenaten in the prime of life.

Photo: Courtesy, Agyptische Abteilung, Staatlichen Museen, Berlin.

129. HEAD OF A KING. Plaster. Height 8 in. Excavated by D.O.G. at El-Amarna, 1911–13. Later reign of Akhenaten. At the former Berlin Museum (Reg. No. 21,354).

The angle from which the photograph has been taken exaggerates the triangular shape of the face. This mask is almost certainly a study of Akhenaten in the later years of his life, shown wearing the Blue Crown. The pronounced lines running from the alae of the nose to the corners of the mouth are a characteristic feature of his portraiture (cp. No. 109).

Photo: Courtesy, Agyptische Abteilung, Staatlichen Museen, Berlin.

130. KING SMENKH-KA-RA AND QUEEN MERT-ATEN(?). Painted limestone. 8¼ x 10 in. Purchased at Giza, 1900, perhaps from Memphis. Co-regency of Akhenaten and Smenkh-ka-ra(?). At the Berlin Museum (Reg. No. 15,000).

This plaque in sunk relief, probably for inlaying in a mud-brick wall, shows a young king leaning languidly on his staff with the wind fluttering the streamers of his dress, while his queen holds out a bouquet for him to smell. The spirit, subject-matter and treatment are entirely in the later syle of the period (cp. No. 154): the figure of the king is admirably drawn and carved; the queen is less happily portrayed. Their portraits differ distinctly from those of Akhenaten and Nefert-iti, and the pair have therefore most plausibly been identified as the little-known Smenkh-ka-ra (cp. No. 140) and his Queen, Mert-aten (cp. No. 136).

Photo: Courtesy, Agyptische Abteilung, Staatlichen Museen, Berlin.

131. SCULPTOR'S MODEL RELIEF. Limestone. 8¼ x 6 in. Acquired ex-Wilbour Collection, 1916; originally from El-Amarna. Later reign of Akhenaten. At Brooklyn (Reg. No. 16.48).

The rapidity with which the city of Akhet-aten had to be built upon a virgin site must have taxed the resources of the craftsmen to the utmost and meant that a good deal of half-trained labour had to be employed upon the various undertakings. To meet the need, master-craftsmen produced models giving patterns of the various architectural and inscriptional details for copying by apprentices and illiterate workmen. In addition, a number of reliefs were made by the master sculptors giving the 'official' portraits of the royal family for the guidance of the sculptors and painters decorating the various tombs and buildings under construction. Such models must have been usual at all periods, but few now exist, though the special conditions at El-

Amarna have been more favourable to the survival of a number of such trial-pieces and models. The one illustrated here is obviously by an authoritative hand for constant reference, as the hole for a suspending cord suggests. The portraits, presumably of Akhenaten and Nefert-iti, have been clearly distinguished on different scales as is normal, and show more than usual mastery in the drawing and carving. The line running from the nostril to the outer border of the mouth (cp. No. 129), fainter in the case of the King, the folds under the chin and the carefully defined collar-bones are all characteristic.
Photo: Courtesy, Brooklyn Museum, New York.

132. SCULPTOR'S TRIAL-PIECE. Limestone. 9 x 7 in. Excavated by Flinders Petrie at El-Amarna, 1891–2. Former Amherst Collection. Early reign of Akhenaten. Collection of Mr. Albert Gallatin, New York.

This specimen illustrates the extreme style of the early years of the reign. The features of the King have been exaggeratedly represented in what is a virtual caricature.
Photo: Courtesy, Brooklyn Museum, New York.

133. A KINGFISHER IN THE MARSHES. Gouache on thin plaster over mud-brick. 12½ x 15 in. From a room in the Northern Palace at El-Amarna. Reign of Akhenaten. After the facsimile by Nina M. Davies.

A chamber opening on to a porticoed court, with a water-garden in its centre, was decorated with one continuous scene, after the manner of a wallpaper, showing bird life among the papyrus-thickets growing out of the mud-fringed water. How the scene was completed is conjectural since only the lower parts of the walls remained. In this fragment, the Pied Kingfisher swoops down to make his catch. The execution is based upon a naturalistic intention, though still not entirely free from the normal conventions of Egyptian painting—the water, for instance, is still represented as an area of blue zigzags. But far more than usual, the artist has designed with his brush, building up the forms with skilful and subtle brush-strokes and by this technique representing texture also. The marsh-plants creeping over the verge of black mud are entirely represented by a fluid brush.
From Davis and Gardiner: 'Ancient Egyptian Paintings,' Pl. LXXVI, by Courtesy of the Oriental Institute, Chicago.

134. A SHRIKE. Gouache on thin plaster over mud-brick. 5 x 6¾ in. From the same room as No. 128. After the facsimile by Nina M. Davies.

A detail from the same scene as No. 128, showing a shrike painted with a full brush in the same sketch-like technique.
From H. Frankfort and Others: 'The Mural Paintings of El-Amarneh,' Pl. IX, by Courtesy of the Egypt Exploration Society, London.

135. HEAD OF KING SMENKH-KA-RA(?). Yellow quartzite. Height 7 in. Excavated by Eckley B. Coxe Jr. Expedition, University of Pennsylvania, at Memphis, 1915. Co-regency of Akhenaten and Smenkh-ka-ra(?). At Cairo (Ent. No. 45,547).

This head, both in its technique and style, clearly belongs to the Amarna age, yet the features do not seem to represent Akhenaten, nor are they at all like those of Tut-ankh-amen. It has been assumed, therefore, that this head represents the co-regent Smenkh-ka-ra. It is in the restrained, naturalistic style of the later Amarna period.

Photo: Courtesy, Cairo Museum.

136. LID OF CANOPIC JAR OF MERT-ATEN(?). Calcite, eyes inlaid. Height 7 in. Excavated by Theodore Davis and S. A. at Thebes, 1907. Later reign of Akhenaten. At Cairo (G. No. 3610).

Four canopic jars (cp. No. 152) with human-headed lids, similar to the one shown here, were found in a small cache in the Valley of the Tombs of the Kings at Thebes containing the desecrated burial of an unidentified Amarna king. These jar-lids have been variously identified as representing Queen Tiy, Akhenaten and Smenkh-ka-ra. There is little doubt, however, that they were originally prepared as part of the funerary equipment of one of the daughters of Queen Nefert-iti and later adapted for the burial of the unidentified king. The most likely candidate among the princesses is the eldest daughter, Mert-aten. It is probable, therefore, that these jar-lids date to the early years of Akhenaten's reign.

Photo: Courtesy, Cairo Museum.

137. STATUE OF A YOUNG KING. Painted limestone. Height 7½ in: Excavated by E.E.S. in ruins of a house at El-Amarna, 1923. Later reign of Akhenaten(?). At Brooklyn (Reg. No. 29.34).

The uninscribed statuette has been identified as representing Akhenaten. It seems to portray a rather younger monarch, however, and it may well be of Smenkh-ka-ra, or perhaps of Tut-ankh-amen. The difficulties in the way of a precise identification from physiognomy alone, when other factors are absent, are so great that the matter is best left in abeyance. The style seems to belong to the later half of the reign of Akhenaten.

Photo: Courtesy, Brooklyn Museum, New York.

138. STATUE OF A KING HOLDING AN OFFERING-TABLE. Painted limestone. Height 15¾ in. Excavated by D.O.G. at El-Amarna, 1911–13. Later reign of Akhenaten. At Cairo (Ent. No. 43,580).

The king, who in the absence of an inscription is identified as Akhenaten on physiological grounds, stands with feet together, in an attitude more usual in Egyptian statues of women, and holds an offering-table containing lotus bouquets, trussed ducks, and loaves carved in low relief. The Blue Crown, made separately and painted its usual blue colour, does not appear to fit and may have belonged to another statue.

Photo: Courtesy, Cairo Museum.

139. STATUE OF AKHENATEN(?) SEATED. Yellow steatite. Height 25½ in. Former Salt Collection, 1826. Provenance uncertain. Perhaps early reign of Akhenaten. At the Louvre (Inv. No. 891). Seat and lower part of legs restored.

The king was originally represented as seated upon a cushioned chair of state, with his queen, whose figure has been broken away, except for her left hand, which still clasps her husband's waist. In the absence of any inscription, the king has been generally identified as Akhenaten on physiognomical grounds; and as the British Consul Salt conducted his operations mostly, though by no means exclusively, in the Theban area, it has been assumed that this statue came from Thebes and was therefore made in the early years of the reign before the exaggerated style of the Karnak sculptures had become fashionable (cp. Nos. 107–109) and before Akhenaten had moved his court to El-Amarna.

Photo: Courtesy, Archives Photographiques, Paris.

140. CANOPIC COFFIN OF KING SMENKH-KA-RA. Gold inlaid with coloured glass and carnelian. Height 16 in. Excavated by Howard Carter at Thebes, 1927. Reign of Akhenaten–Tut-ankh-amen. At Cairo (Carter's Reg. No. 226G).

This miniature coffin for containing part of the embalmed viscera of the dead king was found in the N.E. compartment of the Canopic chest of Tut-ankh-amen (cp. No. 152). Altered inscriptions on the inside show that it was originally made for Smenkh-ka-ra, and adapted later for his successor by changing the names in the cartouches. The features were presumably not altered and present a somewhat different physiognomy from that of Tut-ankh-amen, particularly in the longer, straight nose with its absence of a tilted tip. This coffin shows most of the features of a full-sized royal coffin of the period. The featherwork decoration is inlaid with turquoise-blue and lazuli-blue glass and carnelian. A vulture goddess on either side stretches protective wings around the King. The lid does not quite fit nor close properly, suggesting that some distortion was caused during the process of alteration.

Photo: Courtesy, Griffith Institute, Ashmolean Museum, Oxford.

141. STATUE OF TWO MEN AND A BOY. Painted limestone. Height 8 in. Acquired 1911, probably originally from El-Amarna. Reign of Akhenaten. At New York (Reg. No. 11.150.21).

This little group gives some idea of the quality of private statuary during the Amarna period. The pose, showing the principals holding hands, is apparently suggested by contemporary statues of the royal family (cp. No. 117). The affectionate embrace of the child by the left arm of the second man is also in conformity with the sentiment of the time. Apart from the expression and physique of the persons represented, and the soft flowing lines of the carving, there is in the general style of this statuette something of the spirit of the Old Kingdom, a trend that perhaps may have come from a more dominant Memphite influence in the culture of the later Amarna age.

Photo: Courtesy, Metropolitan Museum of Art, New York.

142. STATUE OF AN UNKNOWN MAN. Painted limestone. Height 7¼ in. Excavated by E.E.S. in the ruins of a house at El-Amarna, 1928–9. Later reign of Akhenaten. At Cairo (Ent. No. 53,249).

Another example of private statuary. The owner sits somewhat slumped in his chair holding a lotus bud in traditional style. The realistic, melancholic portraiture, the gaunt physique of the upper part of the body and the slack lines of the lower could, however, belong only to the Amarna age. This specimen should be compared with the statuette illustrated in No. 1 to see what a whole dynasty of artistic development had done to a similar subject
Photo: Courtesy, Egypt Exploration Society, London.

143. STATUE OF A SCRIBE COMPOSING. Steatite. Height 4½ in. Excavated by E.E.S. at El-Amarna, 1932–33. Later reign of Akhenaten. At Cairo (Ent. No. 59,291).

This little group is in the more orthodox style of the dynasty, probably because it was made for a private person with conservative ideas. It represents the owner writing under the direct inspiration of his patron deity Thoth, the god of learning, whose ape crowned with the disc and crescent of the moon squats upon an altar beside the scribe.
Photo: Courtesy, Egypt Exploration Society, London.

144. RELIEF SHOWING FOREIGN SUPPLIANTS. Hard white limestone, traces of colour. 30 x 21½ in. Acquired 1828, originally from the destroyed tomb of Horemheb at Sakkara. Reign of Tut-ankh-amen. At Leiden (Reg. No. C.3).

Asiatic envoys fall down on their backs and faces ' seven times and seven times' before the envoy of the Commander-in-Chief Horemheb. In the background wait the grooms with tribute horses. This scene is in raised relief. Instances occur of raised and sunk relief being used in the same scene from this tomb in order to give additional depth— a revolutionary space concept. The strongly pyramidal composition formed by the envoy and the suppliants imposes order upon a mass of crowded forms, with its internal rhythms of outstretched hands and bearded faces. The intensity of the moment has been well caught and expressed by the same masterly draughtsmanship responsible for the other crowd scenes from the same tomb.
Photo: Courtesy, Rijksmuseum van Oudheden, Leiden.

145. RELIEF SHOWING SOLDIERS ACCLAIMING THEIR LEADER. Hard white limestone, traces of pigment. 27 x 18 in. Acquired in 1932, originally from the destroyed tomb of Horemheb at Sakkara. Reign of Tut-ankh-amen. At Brooklyn (Reg. No. 32.103).

This detail is from a fragmentary scene in which Horemheb is decorated by the reigning king and parades before him with up-raised arms to receive the collars of gold, while his officers raise their hands in mingled admiration and obeisance in the presence of the Pharaoh. In this fragment the right arm of Horemheb may be seen upraised at the extreme right-hand edge. The hands of his followers gradually

thrust up into the upper register in a mounting climax which is reached by the topmost hand of Horemheb himself—a device for focussing attention to the central figure and tying the various diffuse elements of the scene into a unity. At the same time the supreme audacity of thrusting himself out of his proper station in the register is left to the most important figure. The carving of each face almost as if it were an individual portrait is a feature of the sculpture from this tomb.
Photo: Courtesy, Brooklyn Museum, New York.

146, 147. SCENES FROM MILITARY LIFE. Limestone. 21 x 6½ in. Acquired in the Sakkara area, probably about 1821, by J. Nizzoli, from the destroyed tomb of Horemheb. Reign of Tut-ankh-amen. At Bologna (Reg. No. 1889).

These two illustrations are a continuation of the same scene showing a mounted scout riding to report, followed by soldiers carrying a log. The drawing of the horse is more spirited and original than the normal conventions permit (cp. No. 73) and the pose of the rider as he tries to check the fiery animal has been triumphantly rendered. As if in contrast to this airy and exuberant scene, there follows a squad of soldiers bowed beneath the weight of a heavy burden. The expression of back-breaking effort in conveying a troublesome dead-weight is one of the most masterly successes in all ancient art. The sculptor has in some cases misinterpreted the draughtsman's outline, and the mistakes have had to be rectified in plaster which has now fallen away. The avoidance of straight registers in which to contain the various scenes, similar to the earlier compositions depicting hunts in the desert, is a legacy of the earlier Amarna age with its interest in 'cavalier perspective.'
Photos: Courtesy, A. Stanzani, Bologna.

148. RELIEF SHOWING THE BRINGING-IN OF PRISONERS. Hard white limestone, traces of pigment. 43 x 36 in. Acquired 1828, originally from the destroyed tomb of Horemheb at Sakkara. Reign of Tut-ankh-amen. At Leiden (Reg. No. C.1.).

The scene is in sunk relief. An officer falls on one knee to present to Horemheb an important Syrian hostage whom he leads handcuffed and shackled with a rope round his neck. Other prisoners are brought in by companion soldiers, one of whom turns round to adjure his charge. The bottom register contains the upper part of a scene showing captives and gaolers. The careful portraiture of each face should be noted. Like most of the reliefs of this period, this specimen shows an extremely competent designing of the crowd scenes, variety of expression and pose being achieved in individual details, and the whole tied together by the broad massing of pattern and effective composition. The kneeling officer and his reluctant prisoner have been conceived and drawn by one of the supreme artists of the Ancient World, a man who can make the blank spaces of his design as eloquent as the crowded passages.
Photo: Courtesy, Rijksmuseum van Oudheden, Leiden.

149. KING TUT-ANKH-AMEN HUNTING LIONS. Varnished gouache on gesso over wood. 8¾ x 6½ in. From the cover of a painted casket found in the tomb of Tut-ankh-amen and now in Cairo (Carter's No. 21). After the facsimile by Nina M. Davies.

This detail from a scene showing the King hunting lions, illustrates the ability of the Egyptian painter to work on a miniature scale. The lions are being hunted in the Eastern Desert represented by the clumps of desert shrubs scattered in the folds of the ground.

From Davies and Gardiner: 'Ancient Egyptian Paintings,' Pl. LXXVII, by Courtesy of the Oriental Institute, Chicago.

150. KING TUT-ANKH-AMEN DEFEATING SYRIANS. Varnished gouche on gesso over wood. 5½ x 4¼ in. From the side of a painted casket found in the tomb of Tut-ankh-amen, now in Cairo (Carter's No. 21). After the facsimile by Nina M. Davies.

This small detail is from a scene which is more familiar from similar versions sculptured on pylon walls in the succeeding dynasty. Such mêlées, however, had already appeared on chariot-fronts and on one triumphal stela at least (cp. Nos. 74, 94). The King is charging a mass of fleeing foes while battle-stained troops engage in close-quarter fighting and sever the hands of the slain in order to count them. Some of the Syrians are shown full-face as is usual in such representations, but the expression of pain on the faces of the wounded and dying belongs to the Amarna period with its insistence on realism.

From Davies and Gardiner: 'Ancient Egyptian Paintings,' Pl. LXXVIII, by Courtesy of the Oriental Institute, Chicago.

151. RECUMBENT LION OF KING TUT-ANKH-AMEN. Red granite. Length 84 in. Height 44 in. Excavated by Baron Prudhoe at Gebel Barkal in the Sudan, 1835. Latest years of reign of Tut-ankh-amen. At London (Reg. No. 34).

The original plan for the temple of Amen-hetep III at Soleb, contemplated the placing of two lions at the main portal, but only one was put in position before the King's death: the other, this specimen, remained roughed out in the quarry at Aswan. Work on it was not resumed and completed until the reign of Tut-ankh-amen, who died before it could be installed at Soleb. It was King Ay who transported it to the temple of Amen-hetep III at Soleb, whence it was removed along with its companion in much later times to Gebel Barkal.

Photo: Courtesy, Trustees of the British Museum.

152–161. OBJECTS FROM THE TOMB OF TUT-ANKH-AMEN, excavated in the Valley of the Tombs of the Kings at Thebes by the Earl of Carnarvon and Howard Carter, 1922–32, and now in the Cairo Museum. Photographs by Harry Burton of the Metropolitan Museum of Art, New York. The registration numbers are taken from Carter's card-catalogue of the contents of the tomb.

152. LIDS OF CANOPIC JARS. Calcite, details in black and red. Average Height 10¾ in. From the Innermost Treasury, Nos. 266.

These heads, showing the King wearing the striped wig-cover and royal insignia, acted as stoppers to the four cylindrical compartments of the canopic chest within which reposed the four miniature coffins containing the King's viscera (cp. No. 140). They are remarkable not only for their individual qualities of portraiture and monumental serenity, but also for the identity of resemblance which the sculptor has achieved.

Photo: Courtesy, Griffith Institute, Ashmolean Museum, Oxford.

153. INNERMOST COFFIN OF THE KING. Gold and inlays. Height 35 in. From the Burial Chamber, No. 255.

The coffin, made in the form of Osiris the death-god, with the features of the King, is of massive beaten gold and inlaid with obsidian, carnelian, quartz, lapis lazuli, turquoise, calcite and coloured glass. The King wears the long plaited beard of an Immortal and holds the royal and Osirian sceptres. The goddesses of Upper and Lower Egypt in the form of a vulture and a cobra-headed vulture, enfold him in their protecting wings. They are executed in cloisonné-work, all details being inlaid with brilliant colour effect, and show up from a distance against the chased background with startling clarity, as though clinging to the body of the coffin. The overwhelming size, brilliance and opulence of this specimen are apt to distract attention from the exquisite craftsmanship and the superb conception of royalty in all the dignity of death.

Photo: Courtesy, Griffith Institute, Ashmolean Museum, Oxford.

154. KING TUT-ANKH-AMEN AND QUEEN ANKHES-EN-AMEN IN A BOWER. Wood overlaid with ivory. 8¾ x 12¾ in. From the Annexe (storeroom), No. 540.

This relief, which is part of a decorated box showing scenes from the intimate everyday life of the King and Queen, consists of ivory, applied to a soft reddish wood, and carved and stained. The Queen on the right offers a bouquet of flowers to the King as they stand within a kiosk in their garden. She wears a coloured sash around her flowing garments and an elaborately dressed side-lock (cp. No. 122). On her head she wears three uræi-snakes and an elaborate unguent holder flanked with uræi. The King leans forward on his staff to accept the gift. The columns of the kiosk, its canopy and be-cushioned sill are wreathed with garlands and entwining vines bearing bunches of grapes in true Amarna taste. The scene below shows court maidens in bowers picking mandrakes or love-apples.

Photo: Courtesy, Griffith Institute, Ashmolean Museum, Oxford.

155. THE KING'S GOLD STICK. Gold and gilded wood. Height of the figure, 3½ in. Found between outer and second shrines in the Burial Chamber, No. 235a.

This figurine from the King's ceremonial gold staff shows Tut-ankh-amen as a small child and must date to soon after his elevation to the kingship, probably while he was still at Amarna. He wears the blue War Crown and pleated kilt and apron upheld by a belt fastened with a clasp on which his name is engraved. The king is shown with all the chubby features of childhood and not as a rather wizened adult on a miniature scale which was the usual convention.

Photo: Courtesy, Griffith Institute, Ashmolean Museum, Oxford.

156. A ROYAL SHAWABTI FIGURE. Wood, gilded copper implements. Height of whole figure, 19 in. From the Annexe (storeroom), No. 318a.

This figurine, carved in the likeness of Tut-ankh-amen in mummy-wrappings but with his hands partly freed to hold the crook and 'flail' sceptres, is unusual in that it shows the King wearing the War-Crown —a somewhat incongruous garb for the peaceful Osirian realms: only one other figurine showed the King with this head-dress. It is of superior workmanship to many such figurines, perhaps because it was specially commissioned, along with four others, for the King's burial-equipment by the General Min-nekht, as an inscription on it testifies— a circumstance which may explain why the King is shown in this specimen wearing the war helmet of the Commander-in-Chief.

Photo: Courtesy, Griffith Institute, Ashmolean Museum, Oxford.

157. THREE GUARDIAN GODDESSES. Gilded wood. Average height 36 in. From the Innermost Treasury, No. 266.

Three of the four figures of goddesses who protected the canopic shrine containing the King's embalmed viscera are illustrated here, *viz.* Neith, Isis and Selkit. Their heads are turned in such a way that each controls a different field of vision. They are clothed in tight-fitting pleated linen gowns tied at the waist with a ribbed girdle. A fringed cloak hangs down the back, the upper corners being knotted under the right breast. The hair is enclosed in a linen kerchief tied at the nape of the neck so that a surplus falls as a broad pig-tail between the shoulder-blades.

Photo: Courtesy, Metropolitan Museum of Art, New York.

158. MUMMY MASK OF KING TUT-ANKH-AMEN. Gold and inlays. Height 21½ in. From the Burial Chamber, No. 256a.

The mask is fashioned in gold and inlaid with lapis lazuli, calcite, obsidian, painted quartz, carnelian and coloured glass. The King is shown wearing the striped wig-cover with the cobra and vulture insignia of Upper and Lower Egypt on his brow. Around his neck is a funerary 'hawk' collar. The ears are pierced to receive the ear-rings of youth, but when first found these holes were obscured by discs of gold foil. Beneath the chin is the tenon for the attachment of a long Osirian beard. There seems little doubt that this mask is an extremely faithful portrait of the King, idealised by the sculptor into the calm lineaments of an Immortal.

Photo: Courtesy, Griffith Institute, Ashmolean Museum, Oxford.

159. STATUE OF KING TUT-ANKH-AMEN AS THE GOD HORUS. Gilded wood, eyes inlaid. Height 32 in. From the Innermost Treasury, No. 275c.

The King is represented as Horus-son-of-Isis wearing the Red Crown and about to harpoon and enchain the Typhonian enemy in the form of a hippopotamus in the marshes of Lower Egypt. He poises in a light papyrus skiff with his right arm raised for the fatal stroke. Sadly ruined specimens from the tombs of earlier kings show that the form of such statues was already well established at least by the middle of the Dynasty. The treatment here though is in the style of the late Amarna period with the heavy breasts and hips, slender limbs and garments bellying out as though filled with a wind.

Photo: Courtesy, Griffith Institute, Ashmolean Museum, Oxford.

160. BACK PANEL OF THE KING'S THRONE. Wood overlaid with gold and inlays. 21 x 21 in. From the Antechamber, No. 91.

In spite of the Amen-form of the King's name, this relief in subject and treatment is wholly in the intimate style of the Amarna period, suggesting that under Tut-ankh-amen, there was no proscription of the Aten faith, merely a relegation. The pavilion within which the scene takes place, and which frames it, is a typically florid construction with its elaborate columns and the sun-and-cobra motive of its deep frieze, broken to allow the Aten to shine through with its caressing and life-giving rays. The King lolls on his be-cushioned throne wearing an elaborate Atef-crown and ceremonial collar : his feet rest upon a padded footstool. Ankhes-en-amen, wearing the crown of a principal queen leans forward to anoint him with unguent from the bowl which she carries in her other hand as though preparing him for his coronation. Behind her is a stand on which reposes a formal bouquet, shown according to the conventions of Egyptian art as though seen in plan upon a side elevation. The relief is carved in wood and overlaid with sheet gold. The Queen's garments are of silver which has tarnished with age. All the details are inlaid in purple faience and polychrome opaque glass, presenting a total effect of unparalleled splendour more in keeping with the work of a jeweller than a joiner.

Photo: Courtesy, Griffith Institute, Ashmolean Museum, Oxford.

161. SARCOPHAGUS OF KING TUT-ANKH-AMEN. Quartzite, covered with a red wash, details in colour. Height 58 in. Still *in situ* in the Burial Chamber, No. 240.

This sarcophagus seems to be an adaptation of an Amarna design, since the fragmentary specimen made for the Princess Maket-aten had a figure of Nefert-iti at each corner. Guardian goddesses at the four corners of the sepulchral chest had already appeared on a canopic box as early as the reign of Amen-hetep II. In this sarcophagus, the goddesses are shown winged, an innovation that was doubtless suggested by the outstretched protecting wings of Ra-Herakhty who appears at each corner of the damaged canopic chest of Akhenaten. Where this sarcophagus differs from all preceding examples is in the placing of the goddesses medially at the direct corners so that the spine of each lies along the line of the two planes at right angles, betraying a space-concept outside the instincts of the Egyptian artist. That it was felt to be strange is seen in the placing of the goddesses on the similar sarcophagus of Horemheb, where they have been carefully disposed so that two are fully carved on each long side, two arms only being represented on each shorter side.

This view of the N.E. corner of the sarcophagus shows the goddess Selkit, standing with arms and wings outstretched like the guardian angel of Christian iconography. The goddesses are sculptured with the features of the Queen (the resemblance is particularly marked to the head of the princess illustrated in No. 109. seen in profile), the bodies being carved in very high relief which takes on almost the quality of sculpture in the round. The artist has not attempted to step too far outside the bounds of Egyptian artistic convention—while he has been at pains to carve a left and a right foot, his carving of the hands is inconsistent with the facing outwards of the figure, though the model-ling of the collar-bones and shoulders and arms has resolved the anatomical distortion. This figure, in fact, very clearly reveals the symbolical nature of Egyptian formal expression. The artist wishes to convey the idea of protection and has assembled his elements in such a way as to define this most cogently—the goddesses face out-wards, but turn their hands inwards. The carving must be dated late in the reign of the King, since the lid was unfinished at his death.

Photo: Courtesy, Griffith Institute, Ashmolean Museum, Oxford.

162, 163. STATUE OF A SERVANT CARRYING A JAR. Box-wood. Height 5¼ in. Former Alnwick Collection (No. 752), originally acquired about 1816, probably from the unlocated tomb of Mery-ptah at Thebes. Later reign of Amen-hetep III. At Gulbenkian Museum of Oriental Art, Durham University.

The young Nubian carries a heavy jar which originally contained unguent, and is closed by a lid (not shown here) pivoting on a peg. Certain details, such as the eyes, the necklace with Bes-amulet, and the tufts of hair are indicated with pigment: the girdle over the loins is gilded. This statuette is unusual for the novelty of its pose. The figure executes a twisting movement around a central axis, as though the backbone turned in two different planes. This unusual feeling for space as an entity was probably subconscious and came as a result of realistically attempting to show some of the tensions and displacements caused in the anatomy of a person carrying a heavy and unequally distributed load. The *contraposto* of the upper part of the body is repeated in the pose of the legs, so adjusted as to show the whole weight taken on the right foot. There exist in other collections one or two servant figurines, almost certainly by the same hand, which show a similar unsymmetrical balance.

Photo: Courtesy, Dr. M. F. Laming Macadam, Durham.

164, 165. STATUETTE OF A YOUNG GIRL. Ivory, traces of paint. Height 3¼ in. Acquired 1940, ex-Collection of Howard Carter. Probably from Thebes. Reign of Tut-ankh-amen(?). At Brooklyn (Reg. No. 40.126).

The wig is carved in some detail to represent the heavy braids of hair and thickly painted in black. There are traces of red paint on the lips. The lug on the top of the head, simulating an unguent-cone, is perforated laterally as though to take a suspending cord, though it is doubtful what the exact purpose of this little figurine was. Despite the somewhat costly material and the skill and care in carving certain details, it is evident that this statuette is no more than a charming trinket, expressing a sophisticated rather than a profound taste.

Photo: Courtesy, Brooklyn Museum, New York.

166, 167. GIRL WITH A BIRD. Wood. Height 6 in. Acquired by J. Nizzoli about 1821, probably in Sakkara area. Late XVIIIth Dynasty. At Bologna (Reg. No. 1859).

The girl wears an elaborate unguent-container(?) on her head and holds a fledgling to her breast in her right hand while she adjusts her coiffure with her right hand. The pose and expression are poetically contrived, perhaps even deliberately suggesting a contemporary love-song. This object was almost certainly a mirror-handle.

Photo: Courtesy, A. Stanzani, Bologna.

168, 169. THE LADY MI. Wood. Height 6 in. Acquired originally from a tomb at Medinet Gurob in the Faiyum, 1901. Co-regency of Amen-hetep III and Akhenaten. At Brooklyn (Reg. No. 47.120.3).

This figurine differs from the preceding examples in showing the owner wearing the fashionable costume of the day; probably like the ivory statuette No. 165 and companion statuettes found in the same tomb at Gurob, it was originally completed by a necklace, only the anchoring holes of which now survive on either side of the neck. The head has been enlarged out of proportion to the rest of the figure, perhaps to offset the size of the heavy wig. The features have been carved with a good deal of realism in the style of the period, and there is an evident attempt to show the contours of the body beneath the folds of the robe. The inscription on the base gives Mi no formal title of house-mistress and the assumption is that she was a woman of the harim. It is probable, therefore, that despite the elaborate nature of the attire and the formal stance, this figurine is to be regarded as in the same category as the servant statues.

Photo: Courtesy, Brooklyn Museum, New York.

170. TRIAD OF KING TUT-ANKH-AMEN. Painted limestone. Height 34 in. Excavated by S.A. at Karnak, 1904. At Cairo (Cat. No. 42,097).

The re-establishment of the Amen-religion by Tut-ankh-amen called for the restoration of the images of the god, most of which had been destroyed or mutilated in the reign of Akhenaten. This group shows

the Theban triad of Amen and his consort Mut, with the King taking
the place of the child-member Khonsu. The linking of arms behind
the back to show an intimate relationship had already appeared earlier
in the Dynasty (cp. Nos. 68, 69).

Photo: Courtesy, Cairo Museum.

171. STATUE OF THE GENERAL HOREMHEB. Grey granite.
Height 44 in. Acquired in the Memphis area, 1923. Reign of Tut-
ankh-amen. At New York (Reg. No. 23.10.1).
   This votive statue installed originally in the temple of Ptah at
Memphis, illustrates particularly the accomplished work of the period.
The forms are suave and refined in the traditional Memphite style :
the pose of the sitter with his head bent in humility as he writes to
the promptings of his god, is in conformity with the feeling of the
time (cp. Nos. 96, 143). The nose has been restored.

Photo: Courtesy, Metropolitan Museum of Art, New York.

172. STATUE OF KING HOREMHEB AND THE GOD AMEN.
White, veined marble. Height 80 in. Former Drovetti Collection, 1824.
Probably from Thebes. Reigns of Tut-ankh-amen–Horemheb. At Turin
(Cat. No. 768).
   In this unusual statue, the god Amen is shown with the features of
the monarch but on a larger scale than the King, who stands beside
him. The statue has been usurped from Tut-ankh-amen by Horemheb.
It differs somewhat from normal dyads of the Dynasty and recalls
rather the Memphite pair-statues of the Old Kingdom showing a
standing and a seated figure. The pose here, however, is more naturally
arranged and contrived than the majority of such groups (cp. for
instance, the statue of King Sahura and the Coptos nome, at New
York), and the cutting and polish betray a complete mastery of the
medium.

Photo: Courtesy, Museo Egizio, Turin.

173. RELIEF OF KING AY AS A NILE GOD. Hard crystalline
limestone. Height 18 in. Originally from Medinet Habu, Thebes.
Acquired, ex-Forbes Collection, 1950. At Boston (Reg. No. 50.3789).
   This superb fragment comes from the side of the throne of a
colossal seated statue and represents part of the epicene figure of the
Lower Egyptian Nile in a traditional scene symbolising the binding
of Upper and Lower Egypt under the rule of the Pharaoh. The Nile
god is represented as usual with the features of the reigning king; and
the sensitive portraiture is so individual that we may suspect that it
represents a fairly faithful, if idealised, likeness of Ay (cp. No. 112).
Though Ay's two colossi were probably roughed out in the reign of
Tut-ankh-amen, when the building of a funerary temple at Medinet
Habu was started, there is little doubt that they were completed by Ay
in his own likeness : and it is clear that this sunk relief represents the

last flowering of Amarna art. The refined modelling is still controlled by a naturalistic vision and a masterly draughtsmanship, and has not yet developed the rather lifeless suavity of the reliefs of Seti I at Abydos and Karnak.
Photo: Courtesy, Museum of Fine Arts, Boston.

174. UPPER PART OF A SEATED STATUE OF KING AY. White indurated limestone. Height 103 in. Excavated at Medinet Habu, Thebes, by Richard Lepsius in 1845. At Berlin (Reg. No. 1479).

This colossus is one of a pair that originally stood on either side of the entrance to the King's mortuary temple. The tip of the nose has been restored. The King is shown wearing the Double Crown above the *nemes* wig-cover. Despite the huge proportions of the statue, there has been an evident attempt to render the distinctive features of the King—the bulging eyes, heavy chin and thick lips. The craftsmanship is masterly in the Amarna tradition.
Photo: Courtesy, Agyptische Abteilung, Staatliche Museen, Berlin.

175. STATUE OF AN UNKNOWN MAN AND HIS WIFE. Limestone. Height 52 in. Former Anastasi Collection, 1828. Originally perhaps from Thebes. Probably reign of Tut-ankh-amen. At London (Reg. No. 36).

The style of dress and portraiture, and the entirely naturalistic conception are all in favour of a dating to the later years of the Dynasty, and probably to the reign of Tut-ankh-amen, when such sculpture reached its fullest development. The finest of this class of statuary are the damaged head (Cat. No. 849) at Cairo and the closely related fragment of a dyad of the fan-bearer and general, Min-nakht and his wife, also at Cairo (Cat. Nos. 779a and b), which may be confidently dated to this period since Min-nakht held office under Tut-ankh-amen (see No. 156) and probably also under Ay.
Photo: Courtesy, Trustees of the British Museum.

1. Unknown Man

2. Prince Ahmose

3. Queen Teti-sheri

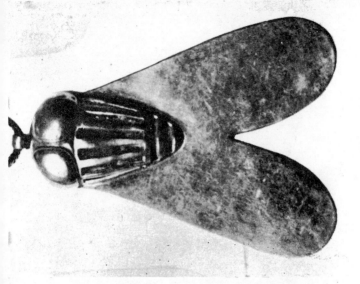

5. Axe-head of King Ahmose

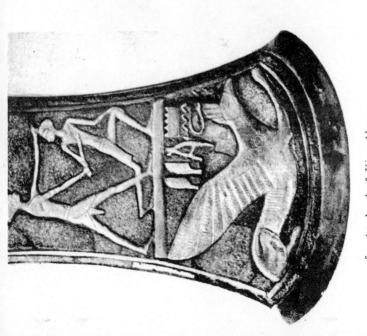

6. Fly of Queen Ah-hetep

7. Head of a Sphinx

8. Bust of a Queen

9. Head of an Unknown King—side view

10. Head of an Unknown King—front view

11. Head of King Amen-hetep I

12. Coffin of Queen Merit-amen

13. Head of King Amen-hetep I

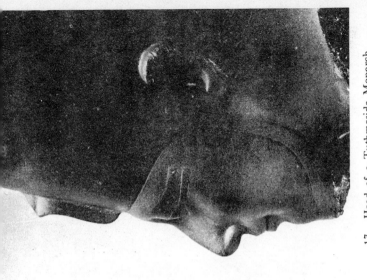

17. Head of a Tuthmoside Monarch

16. Head of a Tuthmoside Monarch

18. Retinue of the Monarch

20. Offering-Bearers

19. Queen Ahmose

21. Queen Hatshepsut Kneeling

J

22. Queen Hatshepsut Seated

23. Granite Sphinx of Queen Hatshepsut

24. Limestone Sphinx of Queen Hatshepsut

25. Queen Hatshepsut

26. King Tuthmosis III

27.　Cretan Tribute-Bearers

28.　A Pet Dog

29. Musicians of the Scribe Amen-em-het

30. Musicians of the Butler Wah

21-22. The Steward Sen-nu-wnu with the Princess Nefru-...

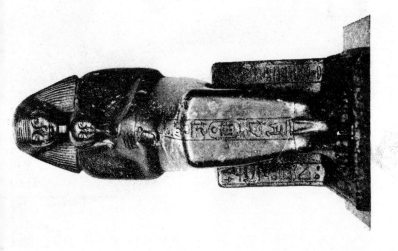

33-34. The Steward Sen-en-mut with the Princess Nefru-ra

35. King Tuthmosis III Kneeling

6. King Tuthmosis III

37. The Vizier User

38. King Tuthmosis III—detail

39. King Tuthmosis III—detail

41. The statue of...

40. Ahmose and his Mother

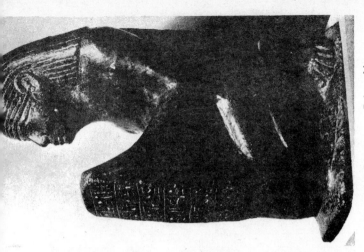

42. The Scribe Roy

43. The Lieutenant Peh-su-kher

44. Wine-Carriers of the Vizier Rekh-mi-ra

46. Brick-Makers

45. Water-Carriers

47. The Local Official Ahmose

48. The Palace Official Sen-nefer

49. King Amen-hetep II and Mertseger

50. The Architect Kha

51. King Amen-hetep II

52. King Amen-hetep II

53. King Amen-hetep II

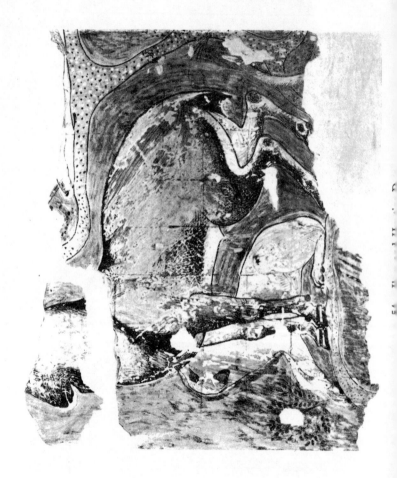

56. Offering-Bearer

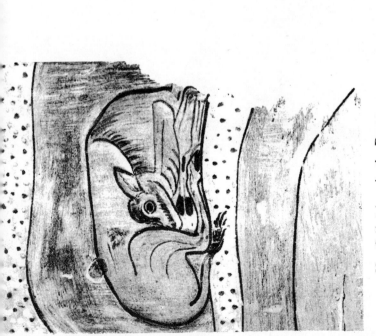

55. Calf Asleep in the Desert

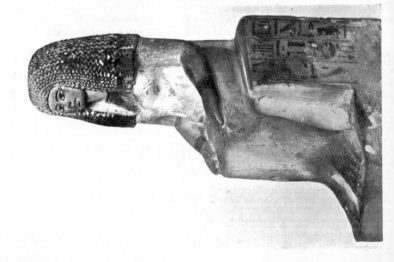

59. Mery-ptah

60. Nubian Captive

63. The Chief Fowler Ptah-mose

64. King Amen-hetep II (?)

65. King Amen-hetep II (?)

66.   King Tuthmosis IV (?)

67. King Tuthmosis IV

68. Sen-nefer and his Family

69. King Tuthmosis IV and his Mother

70. Young Bull Garlanded for Sacrifice

71. Last Farewell at the Tomb Door

72. Guests at a Feast

73. Horses and Mules

75. Harpist

74. Chariot Relief

76. Faience Bowl

77. Faience Monkey

78. King Amen-hetep III

79. King Amen-hetep III

80. King Amen-hetep III

81. The Priest Onen   82. King Amen-hetep III

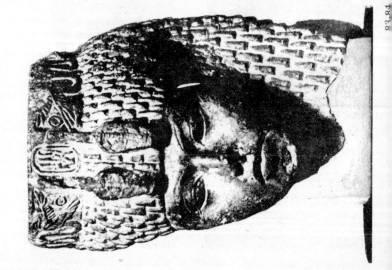

83, 84 Head of Queen Ti

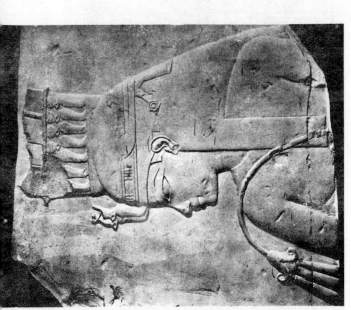

85.　Queen Tiy

86.　Head of a Queen

87. Singers and Dancers

89. Cat Retrieving

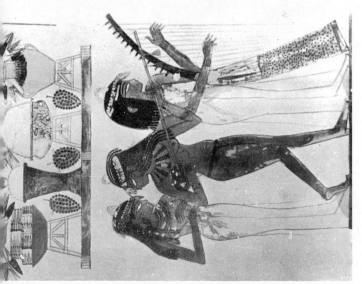

88. Musicians

90.   Jasper Head of a Queen

91. Obsidian Head of a God(?)

93. Mules in the Harvest Field—detail

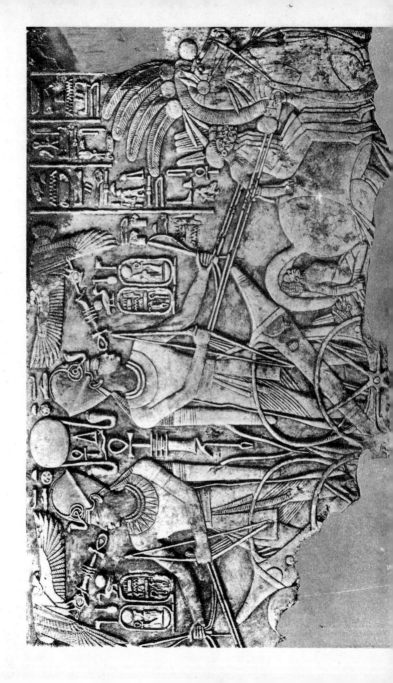

95. Relief from El-Amarna

99. Stone Head

98 Limestone Bust

100. Carnelian Plaque

101. Glass Fish

102. Ivory Grasshopper

103. Ivory Gazelle

105. Offering-Bearers of Ra-mose

106. Mourners of Ra-mose

107-108. Colossi of King Akhenaten

109. Colossus of King Akhenaten—detail

110. The Royal Family Worshipping the Aten

111. An Old Courtier

112. The Fan-Bearer Ay and his Wife

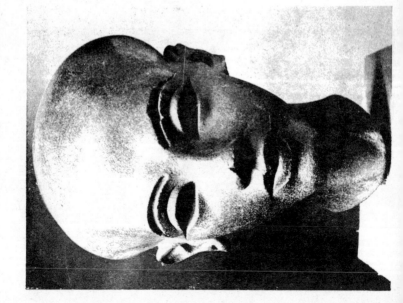

115. Two Young Daughters of Queen Nefert-iti

116. The Royal Family

117. Akhenaten and Nefert-iti

118. Akhenaten(?) Kissing a Princess

119. Unfinished Head of a Queen

120. Portrait Bust of Queen Nefert-iti

121. Head of a Queen

122. Head of a Princess

123. Head of a Court Official

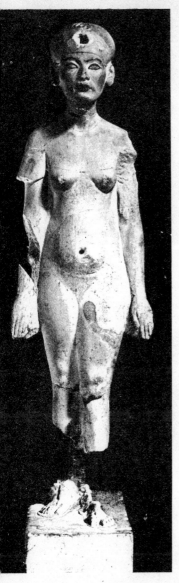

124-125. Statuette of a Queen

127 Head of King Smenkhkare(?)

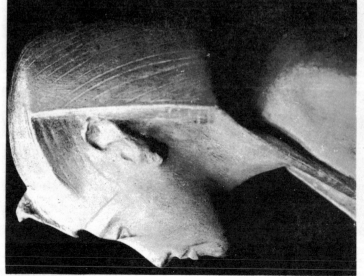

126 Head of King Akhenaten(?)

128. Head of King Akhenaten(?)

129. Head of a King

130. King Smenkh-ka-ra and Queen Mert-aten(?)

131. Sculptor's Model Relief

132. Sculptor's Trial-Piece

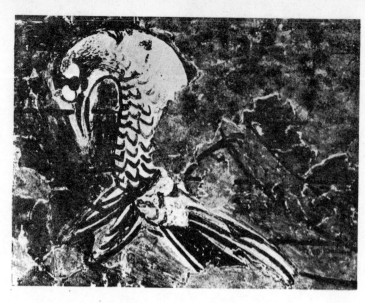

134. Shrike in the Marshes

133. Kingfisher in the Marshes

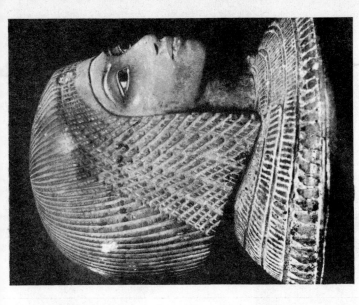

135. Head of Smenkh-ka-ra(?)

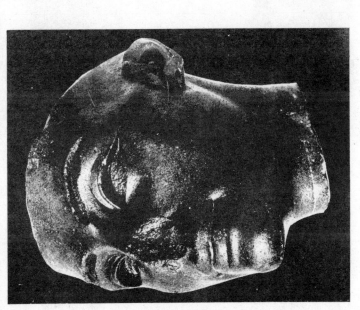

136. Canopic Jar of Mert-aten(?)

137. Young King   138. King with Offering-Table

139. Seated King   140. King Smenkh-ka-ra

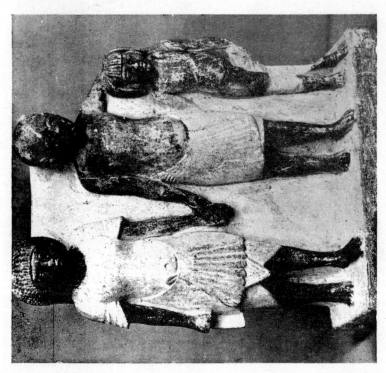

141. Two Men and a Boy

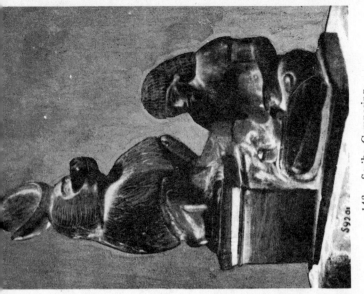

143. Scribe Composing

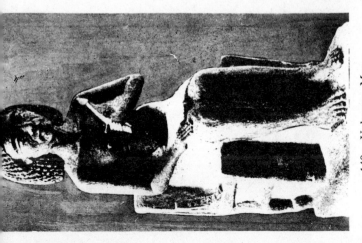

142. Unknown Man

145. Soldiers Acclaiming

147. Pioneers Carrying a Log

148. Leading in Prisoners

149. Tut-ankh-amen Hunting Lions—detail

150. Tut-ankh-amen Defeating Syrians—detail

152. Lids of Canopic Jars of King Tut-ankh-amen

153. Gold Coffin of King Tut-ankh-amen

154. The King and Queen in their Garden

155. The King's Gold Stick   156. Royal Shawabti Figure

157.   Three Guardian Goddesses

158.   Mummy-Mask of King Tut-ankh-amen

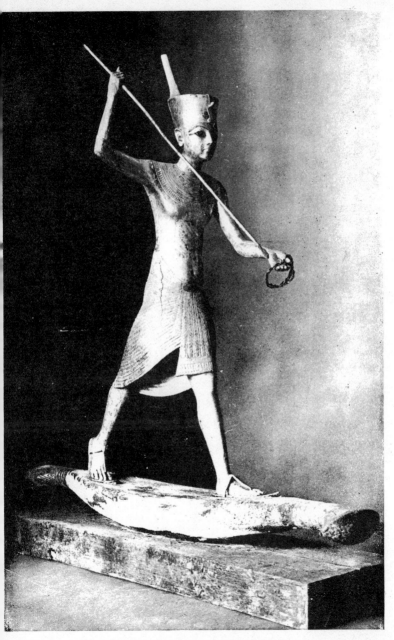

159.   King Tut-ankh-amen as the God Horus

160. Back Panel of a Throne

161.   Corner of the King's Sarcophagus

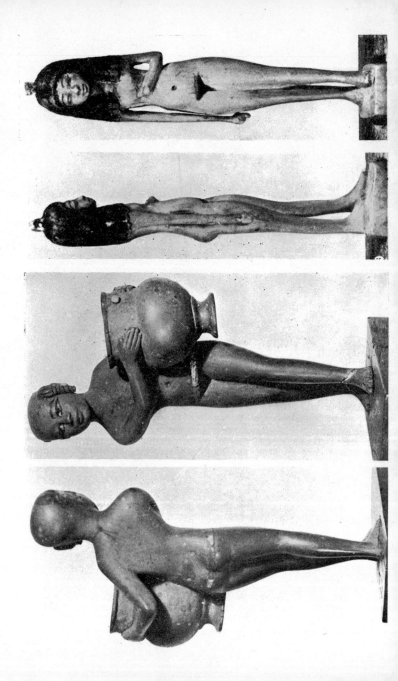

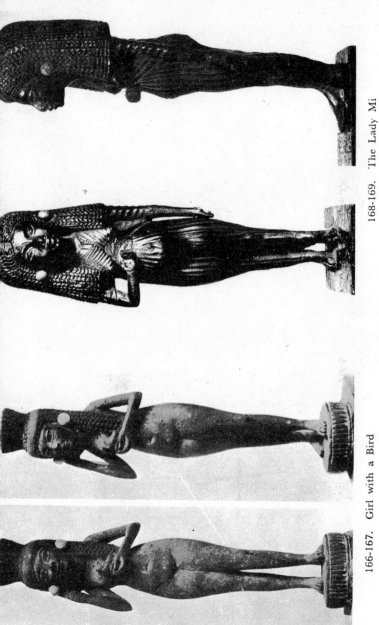

166-167. Girl with a Bird

168-169. The Lady Mi

171. The General Horemheb

172. King Horemheb and the God Amen

173. King Ay as a Nile God

174. Colossus of King Ay

175. Unknown Man and Wife